BLACKBIRDS

*The Glory Days
of Rocky Mount Athletics*

By Lee Pace

John Alexander (76) leads halftime pep talk during 13-6 win over Durham in 1963. Overleaf: Danny Talbott and Blackbirds celebrate 13-7 victory over Raleigh to claim '62 conference crown.

PHOTOS COURTESY NORMA PARKER AND DANNY TALBOTT (OVERLEAF).

BLACKBIRDS

The Glory Days of Rocky Mount Athletics

"Blackbirds: The Glory Days of Rocky Mount Athletics"
conceived and financed by friends of the program.
Committee Chairman: Brent Milgrom,
Metro Consultants, Charlotte, NC 704/552-0113

All proceeds to benefit:
Twin County Museum & Hall of Fame
P.O. Box 8441 Rocky Mount, NC 27804

© 2007 Pace Enterprises Inc.
Chapel Hill, NC 919/933-2082

All rights reserved. No part of this book may be reproduced in any manner
without the express written consent of the publisher, except in the case
of brief excerpts in critical reviews or articles.

ISBN 0-615-1672692495

Book design, layout and production by Lee Pace.
Design consultant Susan Neufeld, Chapel Hill, N.C.

Dust jacket artwork by Jeff Pittman, Asheville, N.C.
www.jeffpittmanart.com

Printed in Canada by Friesens, Altona, Manitoba.

Special thanks to Charles Killebrew for use of his photographs
and to the staff at Braswell Memorial Library.

Dedication

The "Glory Days"—what a great and fun time to have come along. Certainly we were fortunate to have had dedicated teachers, coaches, community leaders, and most of us, great parents. In retrospect, we all can remember an individual from our high school years who had a most positive effect on our adult lives. The person that made a difference in our lives invariably was the one who cared the most. For many of us, Coach Chris Carpenter was that person. "3Cs," as we commonly called him behind his back, was a coach, teacher, and most of all, a good friend to "his boys"—then and now.

So for Darrell, Jimmy, Mike, Purvis, Robby, Wesley, Woody and others that are no longer with us, and for all "your boys" that remain, we dedicate this book to "3Cs."

Plowboy

Blackbird cheerleaders and fans support their team during 34-0 win over Wilson in 1962.

CHARLES S. KILLEBREW COLLECTION, BRASWELL MEMORIAL LIBRARY.

Contents

Foreword by Allan Gurganus   8

Introduction 12
The Town 18
The Foundation 32
The Staff 50
The Star 70
The Edges 82
The Champions 92
East Vs. West 140
Epilogue 146

In Memoriam
Darrell Johnson 150
Jimmy Clack 154

Foreword
Allan Gurganus

"**It was the best of times, it was the worst of times,**" Charles Dickens begins one novel. Concerning those championship seasons of the Rocky Mount Blackbirds, those of us who witnessed the endless wins, who stormed the fields after each game, can claim "It was the best of the best of times."

In recalling high school athletics people tend to make every year a championship season. In this same way, we picture our younger selves as acne-free, driving the family car, dressed up for Homecoming in October tweeds with penny loafers flashing polished pennies. All the girls wore yellow "football" mums, newly pinned in place by dates while their parents flash-bulbed the moment from at least three angles. (Were those flowers called "football mums" for their globe-size or the game that provoked their single use?)

We tend to look better when glancing back over our shoulders, forty years along. And yet, you know what? We were pretty damn cute. We certainly partied hard. Only a few of the very best of us were lost to car-wrecks or a foolish Budweiser idea (that seemed so smart at four AM one Saturday) of walking a live power line across the Tar River.

But one irrefutable Camelot fact remains: Our championship memory is a statistical fact.

The Rocky Mount Blackbirds won just as many games

as our middle-aged memories insist. No, more. To look over the record of wins constitutes a kind of thrill and shock.

People now consider the middle 1960s sweeter, simpler times. Who can argue that? If someone needed you by phone, there was a black six-pound-unit with its own bell. This either plugged in near a table or was sturdily mounted to your Mother's kitchen wall. If the person any caller wanted was not in the house, you just had to call back. Again and again till someone was home and feeling strong enough to actually pick up. Are we better off today? Are we really more efficient? Look at the Blackbirds' 1960s football records and you'll doubt it.

Rocky Mount in those days seemed a unity of tribes. It would be a lie to say we had no racial or social distinctions. It would be wrong to claim that West Haven was not viewed as the crown of creation by those farm families that come Sundays drove up and down before the big white houses that passed for mansions hereabouts. Since I am now somehow a man of sixty, I have some distance on our complicated past. We must admit our High School was then a mostly white institution with a few brave Straight-A black kids transferred from Booker T. to break the barriers so long in place. So our championship team was all pink and blond and brown-haired. I don't remember many brunettes. Tom Parrish?

Booker T. possessed its own ferocious athletic teams. And never did the two great opposing forces meet on a field of battle, Blackbirds vs. the Booker T. Golden Lions. Who knows how **that** championship game would have fared?

What we all have is the memory of our time, of us at our best. It seemed such a prediction for the greatness to come. The band would get there early and the drums started like one great heart, audible from Englewood, even from the railroad tracks crossing over from the Edgecombe side.

We know how it felt to park in that dusty lot, to make our entrance in the cool night air. We can still list our best and fourth best football dates and the names of the teams we played each night. Girls then wore stockings and garter belts under short plaid skirts fastened with gold decorative safety pins. I remember how certain clever horny ten-year-old boys—eager for a glimpse of leg or underclothes beneath those short plaid kilts—would station themselves under certain high bleachers. Once touchdowns were signaled by the screaming from above, the kids left their stations. Otherwise, they concentrated.

As for our winning, our so consistently winning, the athletes did the work but all of us took credit. Even those horrible little bleacher-rat boys, busy with another line of sport under the stands. Wouldn't winning always be like this for us? It would run like that, continuous, inevitable. Surely these countless championships served as the truest prediction of our future lives.

We had a superb coaching staff. I remember Chris Carpenter, not many years past his own gridiron career, and with a neck as big around as my waist, (my waist **then**). Dudley Whitley was as strong and kind and decent as his Dudley Do-Right name. Coach Armstrong, short in stature, wore tortoise shell specs and had a gigantic personality, so warm and winning. Winning was the ticket and a fact.

All we can do now is report what fun it was—to win that often so early in our lives. The coaches were respected, tough minded but fair. Our star athletes seemed to live at the field-house. Their pumped up faith in the chance of another state championship could be felt in the air on those nights in high season.

Basketball games were deafening. Acoustics had never been considered in the construction of a winning team's gym. The din of cheerleading by gorgeous young women—Lindy Brice, Sharon Land and Barbara Nelson still leap to mind whipping black and gold pompoms—chanted us toward still more school spirit. This was a happy way of going deaf. With the buzzer, with the squeals of girls, with the sobbing grunts of half-drunk grown men, the cheer of victory rang on and on. Baseball was another form of winning. But for me those games always seemed "Away."

Football, a harder game to watch than either of the others, brought out the gladiator spirit and half the population. More people attended football games than Baptist services, I bet.

The statistics in this book will affirm a sterling record of accomplishment. What I best remember is the night come fall of 1963 when our tidal wave of victories encountered a first hint, an early turn-signal, that the coming 1960s would not be all Homecoming Queens and Football Mums. The Blackbirds were scheduled to play in Winston-Salem for the state championship. At an early hour in our school day, Principal Edson's intercom unaccountably came alive. We heard the very middle of a radio broadcast. Something was wrong.

"President Kennedy's motorcade in Dallas has come under armed attack. The President has been wounded…" We sat in Latin or Shop Class, numb, disbelieving. This must be a prank or a mistake. As state champions, we were used to mostly winning. We believed in the Danny Talbott vision of true heroes, a boy with all the talent in the world and yet not a bit stuck up. We could not then predict the world incoming, the assassinations that would take out other leaders all too soon.

Even as the President's health was debated, the

coaches must have been off somewhere on telephones. They were deciding whether that same night's football should be played. Coaches decided, rightly, that the game should go on.

The crowd was enormous. People needed somewhere to assemble. Community was something we could believe in. We all needed company tonight. We needed another certainty, this glorious unaccountable collection of great physical talent, the consolations of the game itself.

I remember my date, her tweed coat and its fur collar. There were no bouquets that night. When our high school band played the *Star Spangled Banner*, all heads lowered with a new force of grief. We felt a new and more complicated kind of patriotism. Some essential innocence was fading. Though we couldn't articulate it then, which of us did not feel it? Maybe the world wouldn't be a simple series of games—superlatively played, duly won, and aptly rewarded.

The leader we'd all loved because he was the youngest President ever elected, because he'd seemed, like us, idealistic and forward-looking, had been cut down in his middle forties. And yet, for all the complications awaiting us, despite even the impending deaths of certain heroic Blackbird players in the tangles of Vietnam, this much we can still remember. We must recall it with a simple sort of pride and joy:

The night we lost John Kennedy, our Blackbirds won. ■

Allan Gurganus was born in Rocky Mount in 1947 to a teacher and businessman and graduated from Rocky Mount Senior High in 1965. He first trained as a painter, and his paintings and drawings are represented in public and private collections. His best-selling novel, "Oldest Living Confederate Widow Tells All," was followed by books of short stories and novellas. His forthcoming work of stories is "Assisted Living." Gurganus lives in Hillsborough, N.C., where he is at work on his next novel, "The Erotic History of a Southern Baptist Church."

Introduction

Nearly half a century later, the clicking and clacking of a thousand steel-tipped football cleats scratching the pavement of Hammond Street in Rocky Mount still echoes through the memory banks of some four dozen football players.

There was the sound of the band playing in the distance, the chirps of cheerleaders and the well-wishes from townsfolk lining the way.

There was the ever present aroma of the Rocky Mount tobacco warehouses, of the hot dog and peanut vendors.

There were the orange sparks of the cleats striking the pavement, the glow of the Municipal Stadium lights a few hundred yards on the horizon.

But most of all, there was the *click clack, click clack, click clack*.

"As a boy, I remember it looked like a column of men going off to war," says Brent Milgrom, who attended games in the late 1950s as a junior high student and later suited up in the gold and black of the Rocky Mount Senior High Blackbirds. "They were in their shoulder pads and helmets and I remember how huge they were. You knew as a boy that was something you wanted to be a part of."

Adds Bill Warren, a two-year starter in the early 1960s: "I remember it the first time, I remember the last time. The sound of the cleats. I can hear them today."

The football team dressed in its locker room at the high school bounded by Nash, Tillery and Hammond Streets for those long ago games under the Friday night lights, but Municipal Stadium was a quarter of a mile to the southeast. The coaches could have arranged for bus

Blackbirds celebrate after winning 1963 state crown over Winston-Salem Reynolds (L-R): Ivan Bunn, Jimmy Clack, Monk Reams, John Alexander, Jerry Lundy and Digit Laughridge.

Trains have been at the epicenter of the Rocky Mount economy since the mid-1800s.

transportation from the school to the stadium, but the walk down a couple hundred yards of the railroad tracks served a purpose. It provided ritual and bonding and ten minutes of mental rehearsal for the signal counts, blocking schemes and defensive stunts to come, for the sixteen and seventeen-year-olds from the mill houses beside the Tar River, from the cotton and peanut farms of Nash and Edgecombe counties, from the Colonial and Queen Anne houses along Falls Road and Sunset Avenue to work up a proper state of mental edge.

"They were warriors," says Henry Trevathan, an assistant coach from 1957 through the football season of 1963. "It's like they had an edge of barbed wire. They were polite, they were respectful of their elders. But the process of building a program had matured them mentally, physically and spiritually. There was no small talk. They were a little gruff, a little short. It was all business."

Blackbirds walking the railroad. How perfect.

Rocky Mount was always a bastion in the railroad industry, back from the day in 1840 when a depot opened to service the train connecting Weldon and Wilmington. The town was positioned in the early 1900s as one of the largest rail yards for maintenance for the Atlantic Coast Line, and its Rocky Mount plant ran twenty-four hour shifts to clean the coal-fired engines. The workers were forever covered in coal dust and came to be called "Blackbirds"—ergo the nickname for the local high school team. The precedent runs deeper: The town's first minor league baseball club, the one featuring Jim Thorpe in 1909, was called the Railroaders.

"That walk was the time they got ready to play," says Chris Carpenter, the Blackbird head coach from 1959-64. "Today they would call it 'focusing.' Back then we didn't use words like that. They were just getting ready in their own way to play a game."

"You knew you were getting ready to play a *football* game," says Marion Barnes, a receiver and linebacker on the 1961 and '62 teams. "You knew you were getting ready to have some fun. There was nothing on your mind but playing football."

Rocky Mount in the early 1960s had just over 30,000 citizens, and most of them had football on their minds from August through November. The Cameo and Center Theatres downtown closed on Friday nights; business slowed at Bob Melton's Barbecue up by the Tar River and at Mrs. George's mainstay restaurant downtown, the Carolina Café, as the town migrated to Municipal Stadium and filled it to the brim with upwards of 6,000 fans.

The stadium wasn't particularly well-designed for football, created as it was following World War II in the Works Progress Administration initiative that saw baseball parks built in Rocky Mount, Durham, Wilson and Kinston with the same configuration. Covered grandstands wrapped behind home plate and 90 feet or so up the first and third base lines, and the goal posts for football in Rocky Mount were positioned around third base and in the right-field distance. Bleachers were erected for football along the outfield fences, and many fans simply leaned on the fence to watch the game. There was always bare dirt where the infield was located, yielding a dusty cloud on hot September evenings or a goop of mud in the cold November rain.

It was a spectacle indeed for Rocky Mount home games, until a new stadium was built in the 1980s. The players entered the stadium from a gate behind the west end zone, rallied around captains like Danny Talbott and took the field to the band playing *Hail to the Varsity*.

"It's a shame we don't have that stadium any more," says Bernie Capps, a student manager in the early 1960s and today a physical education teacher and athletic trainer at Rocky Mount Senior. "It was a beautiful, beautiful place. It was intimidating for the opposition. It was loud. It gave you chills."

Rocky Mount was unbeaten at home over three seasons from 1962-64, a period that included back-to-back state 4-A titles in 1962-63 and a near miss in 1964.

"I remember the confidence and the focus on those walks," says Warren, an end on the 1962-63 teams. "The coaches got us ready back at the school and the fans were lining the street, wishing us well. We had a lot of confidence in what we could do and what we couldn't do."

"It had to be a psychological edge for us," says Milgrom, a defensive end in 1962-63 who, like Warren, went on to play college football at the University of North Carolina. "Those dressing rooms at the stadium were pretty rank. For a visiting team to be sitting in that dingy locker room and all of a sudden hear these cleats on the pavement and the excitement building with the fans, it had to have an effect."

They were different times in America and in small towns in the early 1960s, as the strife of Vietnam and the red shadow of Communism, the deathwatch of psychedelic chemicals and the riots and friction surrounding integration had yet to turn the national psyche into an emotional stew. There were no cellphones and no iPods.

Athletics were big in Rocky Mount. Football was particularly important as ACC basketball had yet to stake its claim on the heart and soul of the region.

"As kids, we didn't have video games or the Internet or cable television," says Talbott, the three-sport star generally regarded as the finest all-around athlete to ever emerge from Rocky Mount. "Your life revolved around athletics."

"You grew up reading the sports pages about these legendary players like 'Coal Bucket' Stallings and Bunny Bell," adds David Parker, a two-way lineman on the 1962-63 teams. "Growing up, you absolutely wanted to be a part of football. Friday nights in Rocky Mount, that was what you lived for."

Warren remembers sitting in geometry class in October 1962 as news swirled about the Cuban Missile Crisis; speculation was rampant that the Soviet Union would attack America with nuclear missiles installed in Cuba.

"Okay, if Khrushchev is going to send the missiles, just wait until after Friday," Warren thought to himself. "Wait until after the ball game before you bomb us. Football is just too important …." ∎

Sunset Avenue, looking east from a couple of blocks away from the Main Street intersection.

BRASWELL MEMORIAL LIBRARY LOCAL HISTORY COLLECTION

The Town

The Tar River begins in the Piedmont farmlands between Oxford and Roxboro and flows some 140 miles in a southeasterly direction to the town of Washington, where it changes its name to the Pamlico River. As the river winds its way toward the coast some sixty miles east of the state capital of Raleigh, nature over the centuries created a series of falls and deposited a cluster of boulders that came to be known as "the rocky mound of the Tar." Tuscarora Indians first lived in this region, and settlers from Virginia had migrated here at least by 1732, when the Edgecombe Precinct of Albemarle County was established. They used the river's natural transportation powers to move corn, wheat, tobacco and pork toward markets in Tarboro, Washington and beyond.

Citizens in the western part of the county found it difficult to travel to the county seat of Tarboro to conduct business, so a new county was created in 1777 and named for Brigadier General Francis Nash, who had been killed that year in the Battle of Germantown. By 1816 enough settlers were hunting, fishing and farming the lands that a post office was established and named "Rocky Mount."

The town first embraced the milling business, as the falls in the river were harnessed and provided energy to grind the grain and spin the cotton from the farmland. Battle's Mill was opened in 1818 and became the state's second mill in operation; years later it became Rocky Mount Mills, and a village of small dwellings and a superintendent's house grew up around it as the mill processed the prodigious amounts of cotton from the hinterlands of Edgecombe and Nash counties.

One of the town's early prominent citizens was

The view of West Main Street with the train tracks running north and south, separating Nash and Edgecombe counties.

BRASWELL MEMORIAL LIBRARY LOCAL HISTORY COLLECTION

RM-2 Cotton Mill and Falls on Tar River, Rocky Mount, N. C.

The falls in the Tar River were first harnessed in 1818 when Battle's Mill opened, becoming North Carolina's second mill in operation; years later it became Rocky Mount Mills.

Bennett Bunn, who owned several thousand acres of cotton land. In 1830, Bunn built a brick manor house in the Federal style overlooking Tar River and Stoney Creek. The house is called Stonewall (after the wall built from stone quarries from the Tar River) and today is on the National Register of Historic Places. Another was Nick Arrington, the wealthy planter known for his cockfighting prowess. Legend has it that Arrington took his gamecock to Mexico to challenge Mexican President Santa Anna and came home with $100,000 in gold.

The thriving mill business attracted the railroad industry, and a new depot opened in 1840 to service the Wilmington-to-Weldon route, which at 161 continuous miles was the longest stretch of railroad in the world. The Raleigh-to-Tarboro stage coach route made Rocky Mount an exchange point between rail and stage travelers, and workers from the Atlantic Coast Line began flocking to town in 1903 after a new passenger depot was opened. The red brick, Romanesque revival style building is one of last remaining depots in Eastern North Carolina and today is home to the Amtrak station and the Rocky Mount Area Chamber of Commerce.

The town incorporated after the Civil War in 1867, and in 1872 it sported twenty-one bars and one church. Its next evolutionary chapter occurred in the early 1880s and was built around the need for Duke Tobacco Company to find steady supplies of bright-leaf tobacco to whet the nation's appetite for cigarettes and cigars. Tobacco replaced cotton as the region's top cash crop, and four tobacco warehouses were operating in Rocky Mount in 1895. The town's first bank, the Bank of Rocky Mount, was founded in 1889, and its second financial institution was appropriately named Planters Bank and opened in 1899 to service the new wealth and commerce emanating from the tobacco business. Peoples Bank was founded in 1930, and Planters and Peoples were the primary financial institutions for decades in mid-century until merging in 1990 to form Centura Bank.

"Rocky Mount had three stocks of people, three cultures," says Henry Trevathan, a native of the small town of Fountain in Pitt County and a coach and teacher at Rocky Mount from 1957 through the spring of 1964.

"You had the railroad people. Down through history, railroad people have had strength and character. They're a tough bunch.

"You had the mill people. The best teams in the state were from mill towns, and the best players in any town were mill kids. The best athletes from Rocky Mount were from that side of town.

"And then you had the tobacco crowd, the farm people. Hard work? I think they knew something about hard work."

Many of the players who formed the nucleus of the 1962-63 championships teams grew up in the shadow of Rocky Mount Mills—among them Danny Talbott, Jimmy Clack, Digit Laughridge, Monk Reams, Jimmy Arrington, Billy Warren, J.C. Warren and Craig Quick.

"All those kids went to Wilkinson Elementary School," says Bert Carter, also a Wilkinson student. "Every spring we'd have a field day, and all five elementary schools in Rocky Mount would come together for various games and competitions. Wilkinson always won first prize. We had the best athletes in town."

The mainstays of the business community began taking root: William Soden established a shoe shop in 1866 and W. Soden and Sons operated more than a century until 1970. Epstein's Gents Furnishing Store opened in 1905 at the corner of Tarboro Street and Main. Rosenbloom-Levy opened its clothing store in Tarboro in 1910 and expanded seven years later with a Rocky Mount outpost. The Ricks Hotel was completed in 1900 across the street from the railroad station and was a graceful addition to the architecture until its demolition in 1970. The Atlantic Coast Line helped underwrite the construction of a YMCA just across from the railroad depot; the facility opened in 1911 at a cost of $30,000, the basement including a bowling alley and the upstairs having sleeping quarters for the railroad personnel. Two favorite eating establishments in downtown Rocky Mount were the Central Café on West Thomas Street and City Lunch at the corner of Main and Marigold streets.

A growing town needed recreational facilities, and Benjamin Bunn, son of Bennett, was among the leaders who conceived and built Benvenue Country Club on land the Bunn family owned about two miles north of town. Bunn was smitten with the name "Benvenue" when he read it a Sir Walter Scott poem, *The Lady of the Lake*. The word is derived from a mountain in Scotland, and Bunn named his estate Benvenue and regaled in its peaceful and restorative qualities. Donald Ross, the Scottish golf architect headquartered in Pinehurst, came east to design the golf course, which opened in 1922.

Rocky Mount developed its tastes and favored pastimes, among them dancing, barbecue and baseball.

The idea for a dance to entertain friends from neighboring counties was hatched in 1870 and from this embryo grew one of North Carolina's most esteemed social events and traditions. The dance, or "German" as cotillions and balls were called at the time, was held each June and in 1900 it fell under the auspices of the newly formed Carolina Cotillion Club. The June German was held in Rocky Mount's tobacco warehouses and drew visitors from across Eastern North Carolina. Womenfolk brought out their finest linen, china and silver for the

One of Eastern North Carolina's most prestigious and popular social events was the June Germans.

midnight supper and the men donned tuxedos. During the 1930s heyday of the "big band sound," musicians like native son Kay Kyser, Hal Kemp, Ozzie Nelson, Artie Shaw, Little Jack Little, Jimmy Dorsey and Vincent Lopez played at the June German.

English colonists in the lower James River settlements of Virginia developed the art of cooking pig over an open fire by the late 1600s as word spread through the trade routes of the technique being used by Indians of the Caribbean. Residents of Eastern North Carolina then learned the process and were cooking meat over large oak or hickory logs in the early 1700s. William Byrd of Virginia noted in a 1728 survey of the border land between the states that "inhabitants of North Carolina devour so much swine's flesh that it fills them full of gross humors."

Bob Melton was born in 1872 in Nash County and by the age of twelve had become an expert in cooking pig. He was originally in the mercantile and horse-trading business, but he loved to cook so much that by 1922 he opened a small shed along the banks of the Tar River to sell his succulent pig. Two years later, he christened a restaurant on the spot and began building his reputation as the "King of Southern barbecue." Melton established the tradition now well established in the fabric of life in Eastern North Carolina of finely chopping the smoked pork with a sauce of vinegar, salt, black pepper and red pepper. Guests came from near and far to eat barbecue, Brunswick stew, slaw, potatoes and hush puppies and drink the sweet tea made from water drawn from a natural spring. Melton's airy dining room, offering a great view of the Tar River, was open until floods forced the restaurant to close in 1999.

Professional baseball came to Rocky Mount in 1909 when the Railroaders took the field in the Eastern Carolina League against teams with nicknames like the Tobacconists (Wilson), the Sailors (Wilmington) and the Highlanders (Fayetteville). Jim Thorpe, an All-America in football at the Carlisle Indian School in Pennsylvania in 1908, came south for the summer to pitch and play first base and outfield, earning a salary of twenty-five dollars per week. He returned in 1910 and then was traded to

City Lunch and Blue Bird Taxi were among the fixtures on the Main Street block just south of Marigold St.

Fayetteville. Two years later, Thorpe won two gold medals in the 1912 Olympics in Stockholm, and his triumph in the decathlon earned him the mantle as the greatest athlete in the world. Soon after, however, the medals were stripped because amateur athletic officials felt his baseball employment back in Rocky Mount made him a professional. Thorpe said he was only doing what he knew other "amateur" athletes to do—play one sport for money and another for competition only—but he lost his medals nonetheless.

The Eastern Carolina League lasted only through 1910, but Rocky Mount found a major league affiliation with one club or another (including Boston, Cincinnati and Detroit) and fielded a team most years through 1980. Johnny Pesky (1940) and Tony Perez (1962) were among future major league stars to play in Rocky Mount, and Tony LaRussa and Jim Leyland, each of whom would become outstanding managers, were catchers on the 1966 Carolina League championship team.

Rocky Mount businessmen Nick and Mayo Boddie in front of one of their Hardees restaurants in 1962.

Rocky Mount native Buck Leonard played first base for the Homestead Grays in the Negro National League from 1933-50, batting .342. Leonard joins fellow native Eastern North Carolinians Gaylord Perry (Williamston) and Jim "Catfish" Hunter (Hertford) in baseball's Hall of Fame in Cooperstown. Today Buck Leonard Park sits at the corner of Raleigh Road and Grace Street in Rocky Mount.

Among early notables from Rocky Mount were Kay Kyser, who was born in 1906 and went on to star in radio, movies and television; Bill Murray, born in 1908 and a 1927 Rocky Mount High graduate who coached Duke University to three straight ACC football titles from 1960-62; Thelonious Monk, a jazz musician born in 1917 and often regarded as the founder of "bebop;" and Howard Turner, a four-year letterman at N.C. State from 1943-46 who went on to a long and successful career in the Canadian Football League.

One of the nation's leading fast-food franchises was

Peoples and Planters Banks were located just a block from one another throughout much of the 20th Century in downtown Rocky Mount.

BRASWELL MEMORIAL LIBRARY LOCAL HISTORY COLLECTION (2).

Buyers and sellers flocked to tobacco warehouses in Rocky Mount (L), then the leaf was processed in facilities like those below owned by China American.

Danny Talbott is presented a key to the city of Rocky Mount from Mayor Billy Harrison (L), while coach Chris Carpenter looks on.

born in nearby Greenville in 1960 when Wilber Hardee began selling hamburgers with a distinctive charcoal-broiled flavor from a homemade stand. Leonard Rawls was a Rocky Mount accountant looking for an investment, and he thought Hardee's enterprise had some merit and discussed the idea with Jim Gardner, a Rocky Mount businessman and vice president of a dairy. They invested in Hardee's hamburger stand in 1961, soon bought him out and moved the business to Rocky Mount, opening a headquarters on Sunset Avenue in 1962. The first store featured red and white tile and soft drinks served from a barrel, and customers flocked to its walk-up windows to order from the simple menu featuring burgers, fries and milk shakes.

Chris Carpenter, the Blackbirds' head coach from 1959-64, remembers the coaches eating Hardees burgers every Sunday night while studying game film. He was pitched by Gardner as the Hardees' executive was trying to find twenty investors to ante up $5,000 each. The company later went public in 1963, selling 37,500 shares at $4 each.

"I told him, 'Jimmy, I don't have that kind of money. I don't *make* $5,000,'" Carpenter says. "He said he'd be happy to sign a note for me. But my wife was pregnant and it was just something I didn't think I should do."

Teenagers in Rocky Mount spent their time playing sports, cruising and dancing to beach music. Local hangouts included the Tasty Freeze downtown and the Soda

Shop, operated across the street from the school by a man named Dick Stankus, who sold a three-pack of donuts wrapped in wax paper for a dime, hot dogs for fifteen cents, Cokes for a nickel and the clandestine cigarette from an open pack for a penny each. There was also the Goody Shop, which was located near the old fairgrounds. A drag race was liable to rev up most any night at the fairgrounds, and Brent Milgrom notes that "Our parents' autos' left-side tires usually wore out first because everyone drove around and round the Goody Shop."

The most unusual social entertainment during the early 1960s was provided by the Sheep's Club, a fellowship named for "the black sheep" uncle of Jep Rose, one of the club's original members. The boys renovated a cinderblock building in the West Haven section of town to use as their clubhouse. The club hosted a number of weekend parties throughout the year with a cover charge of fifty cents per person. They were well received and eventually the Sheep moved their gatherings to the National Guard Armory or Masonic Temple. Crowds upwards of 700 teen-agers from all across Eastern North Carolina came to hear live entertainment from the Tams, Embers, Temptations, Del-Vikings and Maurice Williams and the Zodiacs. Many of the Sheep's Club members were football players and remain close today.

And so as the 1960s dawned and evolved, Rocky Mount was a pleasant town with an essence not much different from towns portrayed on popular television shows of the day—Mayberry from *The Andy Griffth Show* and Mayfield from *Leave it to Beaver*. Humorist Lewis Grizzard once put it aptly: "There are only two kinds of people in this world: Ones that were born and raised in small towns and ones that wish they had been."

"Rocky Mount had a small-town feel, a feeling that this was *the world*," says Rose, a Rocky Mount native, Blackbird athlete in the early 1960s and today a local attorney. "You didn't have the global feel you have today with all the TV networks and the Internet. Obviously, some kids had more money than others, but you never paid any attention to it. Just a very few kids had cars, and of the ones that did, they were old and beaten up. Having a car wasn't a birthright like it seems to be for today's kids."

Much of the town's energy went into supporting its youngsters in youth league sports endeavors and then watching them grow into young adults while playing for Rocky Mount Senior High.

"Blackbird football was the talk of the town," Bill Warren says. "It was a small, tobacco town with railroads. Football moved the town. These young athletes who went out and waged war on Friday nights, it just became a big, big deal to the town." ∎

The Foundation

He insisted they call him *Charlie*. It was not *Mister* Daniels. It was not *Coach* Daniels. It was simply, *Charlie*.

"When you're working with kids, and they call you 'Mister,' you're elevating yourself above them," Charlie Daniels says. "When they called me Charlie, they're looking at me right here in the eye. I can look in their eyes, and you've got them. You're on their level, and they'll do anything in the world."

Daniels worked as program director for the YMCA in Rocky Mount for forty-four years, starting part-time as a teen-ager and continuing through adulthood. "I had the best job in the world," he says. "I loved every one of the kids. I worked sixty-five hours a week for forty years and loved every minute of it."

He administered a wide-ranging program of youth sports activities that many involved credit with building a foundation that helped with the future success of the athletic teams at Rocky Mount Senior High School. The YMCA ran a Midget League football program, Small Fry baseball and Little League baseball. There was also an active Church League basketball program in Rocky Mount. Of the thirty-five players on the 1962 state title football team at Rocky Mount Senior High, thirty-three of them had played in the YMCA's Midget League program, and of the two who did not, one had just moved to town from Kentucky and the other had a medical issue.

Rocky Mount High football coach and athletic director E.E. "Knocker" Adkins congratulates Small Fry League title team in 1952. The team's coach is Billy Pierce, and that's Danny Talbott top row right.

PHOTO COURTESY CHARLIE DANIELS

"Charlie's efforts helped create an atmosphere of success which not only fostered athletic success but countless number of notable adults," says Brent Milgrom, listing North Carolina Governor Michael Easley, Wachovia CEO Ken Thompson, former JP Morgan CEO Bill Harrison and author Allan Gurganus among prominent names who grew up in Rocky Mount in the mid-1900s. Hugh Shelton, former head of the Joint Chiefs of Staff, grew up in the Edgecombe County town of Speed.

"The parents were involved. The programs were well-organized. You knew if you were showing up for a game, there would be an umpire and scorekeeper. There was a sense of structure and discipline. There were certain behaviors you knew would not be tolerated."

E.E. "Knocker" Adkins, the high school coach from 1946-54, gave Daniels and the coaches the offensive and defensive sets to run. Every team knew exactly what the other team was going to do schematically.

"Fundamentals were more important than trickery," Daniels says. "I think that had a lot to do with their future success—they had a great foundation in the fundamentals. We said the heck with batting averages or point totals. It was time to teach."

"We were well-schooled fundamentally, going back to Midget ball and junior high," says David Lamm, a 1963 Rocky Mount Senior High graduate who played high school football through his sophomore year before an injury sidelined him. "We were taught properly. We didn't get many penalties and we didn't turn the ball over. Our running backs knew how to protect the ball long before you heard them talk about it on TV."

The players who came through the program look back today and have a healthy appreciation for the stability the youth league programs provided in their development as athletes and young men.

"You played with the same people from Midget League all the way through high school," says Ernest Bridgers, RMSH Class of '61. "You played the same system. You knew what you were doing and who you were doing it with. That made a huge difference."

Jimmy Daniels, a catcher on the 1963 state champion-

Ken Thompson receives an award from the Optimist Club in 1963. Today he is CEO of Wachovia Corp.

Little League baseball games were always a big draw among parents and townsfolk in Rocky Mount.

ship baseball team, was Charlie's nephew.

"One of the reasons we were so good in high school is we'd been playing together since we were little kids," Jimmy says. "Charlie was really interested in young people and did everything he could to keep them on the straight and narrow."

Danny Talbott, the three-sport star who emerged as a special athlete by the time he was ten years old, remembers the continuity that coaches like Melvin Newell, Bob Williams, Bryant Aldridge, Jack Swenson and Coco Booth brought to the various sports programs.

"We had really good coaches at that level, and many of them were there for years," Talbott says. "They weren't there just because their own sons were playing. They coached for many years past their own sons moving through the program."

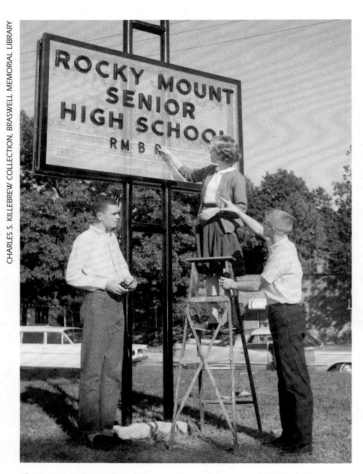

George Watson, Nancy Severance and Chuck Taylor attend to the sign in front of Rocky Mount Senior High, which opened its new facility in 1953.

Rocky Mount High School moved from a building on Marigold Street just east of downtown to a new structure on Tillery Street in 1953, and the previous high school became a junior high named for former principal Robert M. Wilson. The new school, officially named Rocky Mount Senior High, was at the cutting edge of education within the state as it changed its grade structure from eight years of elementary school followed by four of high school to six years of elementary school, followed by three of junior high school and then three of senior high school. It was small in enrollment compared to its competition in the Eastern 4-A Conference. New Hanover High in Wilmington had more than 2,000 students, while Broughton High in Raleigh and Durham High were in the 1,500 student range. Goldsboro, Wilson and Rocky Mount were the smallest with 1,000 or fewer.

"The beauty of the small town was we grew up playing everything together," Lamm says. "Wilson and Rocky Mount were the two smallest 4-A schools at the time. We were the country bumpkins. We used to love to whip the city boys from Wilmington and Raleigh and Durham. We took a lot of pride in that."

Henry Trevathan grew up in Fountain, N.C., a small town just west of Greenville, and has spent most of his life coaching in Eastern North Carolina. He believes the identity of most small towns in the South is defined by

Municipal Stadium was built as a baseball park following World War II but served as the Blackbirds' home football stadium as well.

PHOTO COURTESY BERNIE CAPPS

What It Was, Was Spero At A College Football Game

Spero Kounouklis attended his first college football game in 1933 when Texas played UNC in Kenan Stadium. Much in the mold of Andy Griffith's *What It Was, Was Football,* Kounouklis later recounted his experience at the game in the rapid-fire, broken-English delivery the townsfolk of Rocky Mount knew so well:

"Everybody sat in stand, millions of them. Eat peanuts. Drink pop. Yell like hell. Fellow told me the score, was nothing, no score. Nobody win. Then some fellow on the field, I don't know who he play for, pick up ball that another fellow hand him and start running. All the folks stand up and holler loud more than before. The fellow with the ball he keep right on running, nobody would catch him. The folks, they keep right on yelling. Then the fellow with the ball, he run to the end of the field. I thought he was going home to supper, I was sorta hungry myself, but everybody quit chasing him and he give the ball to the man with white pants. The crowd gone plumb crazy now. Fellow grabs my cap and throw it way in air. I start looking for cap. Fellow next to me say somebody make a pushdown, but I no care. I look for my cap. Pretty soon everybody go home but me. I find my cap filled with peanut shells. Football too rough for me."

their high school football team, and he made a careful study throughout his coaching career throughout Eastern North Carolina of the "larger-than-life" coaching figures that dominated in each community.

"The 1940s, '50s and '60s were a time when the coaching profession was noted for legends," says Trevathan. "A lot of coaches spent their lives in one place, one town. You didn't replace them. If you were an assistant coach, you stood in line and waited twenty years, thirty years until their career was over and there was an opening."

The region had plenty of these "larger-than-life" characters. Leon Brogden won a multitude of state titles in football, basketball and baseball at New Hanover High in Wilmington from 1946-67 and coached future NFL quarterbacks Sonny Jurgenson and Roman Gabriel. Rocky Mount native Buddy Luper was a standout halfback at Duke University in the 1940s who coached Fayetteville High to a share of the 1956 state football title. James "Choppy" Wagner was a 1938 Wake Forest graduate who went on to a three-decade career as football coach and athletic director at Washington High. Frank Mock was a 1934 Davidson College graduate who moved to Kinston, coached for a quarter of a century and won the 1955 state 3-A football title. Clyde Walker was a 1951 Catawba College graduate who began a distinguished career in coaching and athletic administration by coaching Raleigh Broughton High to the 1961 and '66 state 4-A football titles; Walker was then hired by Bill Dooley at the University of North Carolina as an assistant coach and recruiting coordinator. Trevathan himself would leave Rocky Mount after the 1963-64 school year to move to Wilson, where he established a powerhouse at Fike High School with three 4-A titles from 1967-69. Paul Jones was the basketball equivalent of these luminaries with his thirty-eight years of success at Kinston High—eighteen conference titles, two state championships and four state runner-up finishes.

High school athletics were important in each of these towns, football in particular. Washington High football celebrated its centennial in 2006, and former Pam Pack player Bartow Houston spoke eloquently of the school's tradition, known as the "long blue line," in an interview with the *Washington Daily News*.

"Let me tell you about the long blue line," Houston said. "The long blue line is about heroes. We have a lot of heroes in society today; we just don't pick the right hero all the time. We are buffeted with all types of people: Movie stars, musicians and athletes. They are all good ones, but the heroes, the real heroes, don't get their names in the paper or on the television. They do things like loving, raising, teaching and coaching you."

Rocky Mount's entry into the coaching legend camp

was Emery E. "Knocker" Adkins, the Blackbirds' head football coach during two stints through his resignation following the 1954 season. Adkins played center at Duke under coaches Jimmy DeHart and Wallace Wade from 1929-31, began his coaching career in Greensboro and Wilmington and then came to Rocky Mount in 1936. His teams in 1937 and 1940 won the Eastern 3-A Conference titles before Adkins served in the Navy. Following military service, Adkins coached one year under Bill Murray at the University of Delaware, then returned to Rocky Mount in 1946 as football coach and athletic director.

He compiled a 93-28-3 record before leaving to become general secretary of the local YMCA.

"Knocker was a 'knocker,' I guess that's where the nickname comes from," says Bob Williams, the sports editor of the *Rocky Mount Telegram* for fifteen years in the 1950s and 1960s. "He was tough, disciplined, organized, demanded the best and got the best. I don't know that a coach like that today would be accepted for too long. He's from the old school, and once in the while a player got kicked in the butt."

Don Stallings was a tackle as a sophomore and junior on Adkins' teams in 1953-54 and remembers playing without a face mask before the protective gear was installed on helmets.

"If your face wasn't all scratched and torn up, Knocker'd say you weren't using proper technique," Stallings says. "He taught you to block with your head up and go in smiling. One time I had four or five teeth knocked out on one play and all Knocker could say was, 'Great technique, Stallings.'"

Bill Lundy, the boys basketball coach and tennis coach since 1949, was promoted to athletic director for the 1955-56 school year. Clyde "Cleet" Cleetwood, who had been an assistant football coach for Adkins for nine seasons while working also as head baseball and assistant basketball coach, was named head football coach. The Blackbirds had an excellent season, their best in years, and finished 8-1-1. They beat Salisbury, the even-

Homecoming parade in 1963 included a Blackbird mascot riding on the hood of a car (L) and members of Homeroom 118 being pulled by a tractor in front of Chandler's on Main Street. The girls looking at the camera are Linda Melton (L) and Beverly Sue Carmichael. Betty Armstrong is between them in the straw hat.

tual state champion, 18-0 in the second game of the year and lost to Durham 14-13 despite holding the Bulldogs to minus yards rushing. They tied Raleigh Broughton, 6-6. Stallings and Fred Harris went on to play at Carolina and Bunny Bell played at Duke.

Rocky Mount's fortunes took a ragged turn for much of remainder of the decade. The Blackbirds were never bad over the next few years, but they were never great as a succession of four coaches took the helm for one-year stints each.

"Any time a legend steps aside, when it comes to an end, you don't want to follow those people," Trevathan says. "A lull or chaos or something follows it. How are you going to follow Dean Smith? You can't match up to them. You can't penetrate that legacy. You have a hard time doing it *your* way. Too many people are entrenched with the old way."

"The transitions really screwed us up," says Mike Lundy, one of Bill's two sons and a 1960 graduate. "Things were always changing. Some guys decided not to go out for football the next year under the new coach. If the guy before had stayed, they might have come back. It was an up-and-down period, that's for sure."

Cleetwood was promoted to principal at Wilson Junior High after his one year as head coach and next came Johnny Guiton in 1956 for a one-year term. The Blackbirds were 4-6 and 1-5 in the Eastern 3-A Conference.

Ken Yarborough was a three-year letterman at UNC from 1951-53 and a captain his senior year. He entered the coaching business and landed the Rocky Mount job in 1957. One of his assistants was a former Tar Heel lineman named Chris Carpenter. The Blackbirds had a tough year with a 3-7 record and only six points of offensive production the final four games of the year.

Yarborough left to enter private business after one season and former Wake Forest player Don Hipps was named the new coach for the 1958 season. Hipps retained Carpenter as an assistant and hired a fellow former Demon Deacon named Jim Horn. The team was 3-5-2.

One of Hipps' pet plays was a pass called "Ronnie Go Long." Jimmy Mooring was a fullback with the ability to throw the football prodigious lengths, and Ronnie Jackson was a halfback who could outrun anyone on the field. The Blackbirds were trailing Wilson 14-7 with thirty-five seconds left and had the ball on their twenty-seven yard line when Hipps called the play. Mooring moved to quarterback, took the snap in the shotgun formation and ran around in the backfield until Jackson could get downfield. Mooring threw the ball from the fifteen yard line, it traveled sixty-five yards, and Jackson caught the pass on a dead run at the twenty and raced into the end zone. Jimmy Gilbert's point-after secured the tie.

Blackbird cheerleaders lead the team onto the field at Municipal Stadium.

Senior car all fun and games as the "Blackbird Special" heads to Wilmington for 1963 game.

CHARLES S. KILLEBREW COLLECTION, BRASWELL MEMORIAL LIBRARY

"Doug Flutie has *nothing* on the 'Birds," says David Williams, a Rocky Mount graduate in 1963. "That's a great sports bar story and was a classic ending. I was twelve or thirteen that year it was one of those plays you never forget."

Despite this fallow period of only ten wins in three years, the program had two elements of consistency in the persons of Lundy as the athletic director and Carpenter as an assistant coach.

"There's a little continuity beginning, even through the change, change, change," says Trevathan. "Chris is there. Bill Lundy is there. They are the thread. It's not a total sweeping of the house."

"We were able to learn from the earlier teams, the teams that didn't quite get there, but were very, very good football teams," Bill Warren says.

Hipps moved to Charlotte after one season and Carpenter was elevated to head coach. Gradually, the victories started coming. The 1959 team, Carpenter's first, won the league with a 7-3-1 record and was led by Jackson, who took his speed to Chapel Hill to play for the Tar Heels. The 1960 team was 5-5, never putting two wins back-to-back. Then the 1961 team ripped off six wins to open the season, including a 13-12 win over Fayetteville, and finished 8-2-1 with a berth in the state playoffs.

David Lamm and Jep Rose were among the younger boys who took note of the growing prowess of the high school athletic teams.

"As a junior high kid, you looked up to the Blackbirds," says Lamm, who went into the newspaper business in Greensboro and now hosts a sports talk show in Jacksonville, Fla. "You would not dare miss a Rocky Mount Blackbird game. They were my heroes. I think the teams before us set a standard and a tone that carried over. They made sports important. They made it cool to be a Blackbird. There was a period before that where sports just weren't that big a deal."

Rose, a member of the class of 1964, agrees.

"The community was a little indifferent four to five years before the program began to take off in the early 1960s," Rose says. "They were accustomed to not winning. You'd have a winning season but it might be something like 6-4. There was never any real consistency."

The Rocky Mount business community and the townsfolk were always staunch supporters of Blackbird athletes, and a solid foundation of support was there in the 1950s that would explode as the team's fortunes took off in the early 1960s. Groups of up to a dozen townsmen would join the football coaches to watch film on Sunday nights, and the Sportsman's Club met every Monday night, with the head coach showing film from Friday's game and introducing the "Blackbird of the Week."

Betty Armstrong's cartoons graced the pages of the school newspaper in the early 1960s. This one ran the week in 1962 the Blackbirds traveled to Raleigh and won the conference championship.

One of the Blackbirds' most ardent fans was Spero Kounouklis, who emigrated from Greece in the early 1900s and ran the New York Cafe on Tarboro Street in Rocky Mount for years. Spero was pictured in the *Hi-Noc-Ar* yearbook regularly through the 1950s and identified as "honorary coach." He fed players with pre-game meals and once bought new uniforms for the school band. An award was given each year to a ninth grader in Spero's honor who best exemplified his character and school spirit. He was an integral part of the program through his death on Christmas Eve, 1959.

"Spero called the players 'My boys.' They were in his mind and his heart," says Bob Williams. "He rode on the bus to every away game. He helped more boys than anyone ever knew. Some kids came from destitute families, and it was not unusual to find out down the road that Spero had helped this kid or that kid."

Another staple in the largesse of the business community was Lucille George, the proprietor of the Carolina Café on Church Street. The Blackbirds ate many pre-game meals there on their way out of town for road games, always wolfing down a piece of her famous peanut butter pie for the road.

"Mrs. George really looked forward to feeding the boys," Williams says. "She met them at the door, greeted everyone and made them feel at home. She would roam from table to table during the meal, making sure everything tasted right and everyone had enough. She was very devoted."

The community further showed its support for the Blackbirds with its willingness to travel en masse to away games. M.S. Jones was the district superintendent of the Atlantic Coast Line and organized "Blackbird Specials" to Wilmington, Fayetteville, Charlotte and Winston-Salem.

"Road trips were big affairs, they were *events*," says Bert Carter, RMSH Class of 1966. "And it wasn't just students and parents. There where many people with no connection to the high school who enjoyed following those teams. We were seldom disappointed."

Round-trip fares averaged about four dollars for the trip to Fayetteville. The trains might leave at 2:30 in the afternoon for Winston-Salem or at 5 p.m. for the shorter trip to Fayetteville, returning immediately after the game. For the trips to Charlotte for regular-season games against Myers Park and the 1962 state playoffs, the train left Rocky Mount and went to Hamlet, where it picked up a new engine from a different rail company and connected to a second rail line to the west toward Charlotte. Upwards of six hundred people would make the trips. Tom Parrish, a senior center on the 1962 state title team, remembers the rush of riding the team bus to

Chris Carpenter (in hat) waits with his players to address Blackbird fans following 1962 state title win over Winston-Salem Reynolds.

Wilmington along Hwy. 117 and seeing the Blackbird Special train pass it on the adjacent tracks, the rail cars decorated with black and gold and signs mounted exhorting the Blackbirds to victory.

"As a nine, ten, eleven year old, it was very exciting," says Caroline Johnson McCall, younger sister of Darrell Johnson, a football and baseball standout of the period. "The trains were packed and I can remember running up and down the aisles. When we went to Fayetteville, the train crossed Hay Street and stopped and we walked to the stadium. It was great fun."

"We had a tremendous supporting class from this town," says Danny Talbott. "We had more fans at road games than the home team did. It was phenomenal. Car, bus or train—they would find a way to get there."

Carter remembers city buses picking the Rocky Mount fans up at the rail station in Charlotte and transferring them to the school.

"We were riding through Charlotte with several cheerleaders as they led us in the chant, 'Hey hey, we're from Rocky Mount, if you can't hear us now, we'll yell a little louder.'"

Friday morning assembly programs during football season often served as pep rallies, and students planned and executed skits predicting all manner of glorious results to come that night. Bobby "Boris" Pickett's No. 1 hit from 1962, *The Monster Mash*, of course made its way into the skits as a new member of the "Blackbird Graveyard" was readied for interment. Then late on Friday night after another Blackbird victory, a group upwards of 150 students would attend "funeral services" for the just-dispatched opponent. A wooden headstone with "RIP" and the opponents' name was placed in the graveyard beside the football practice field and a poem read to commemorate the occasion.

"We had a lot of fun," says David Williams. "Of course, as much as we were winning, it wasn't hard to get people involved. Rocky Mount was a smaller school and a smaller town then, and everyone rallied around the Blackbirds."

"We had great school spirit," Carter says. "The winning fed the fans, and the fans' emotion fed the winning."

Anne Milgrom Kennedy was a sophomore cheerleader on the JV squad during the 1963 football season when her brother, Brent, was a senior defensive end. A burning memory for her is the day of the Raleigh Broughton game in early November. The Blackbirds had to beat Broughton to win the conference title and advance to the state playoffs.

"The halls at school were covered with posters, and the booster club had made sure that all students were wearing the traditional gold ribbons printed with black," says Anne, who lives today in St. Helana Island, S.C. "We didn't learn much in class that Friday. We were, after all, at the high point of a spectacular season and preparing to play for the conference championship. The varsity cheerleaders prepared the banner through which the players would run on to the field. And to our squad's delight, they requested that the JV squad cheer with them. Well, *almost* with them. We would be stationed in the stands within the parents' section.

"The excitement of cheering at the big game was overwhelming, but I couldn't have imagined that forty-three years later I would still remember the crowd's roar with excitement, the bright lights of the stadium, the cool night breeze and cheering till there was little voice left."

The words come easily, all these years later:
We are the Blackbirds, mighty mighty Blackbirds
Everywhere we go-o, people want to know-o
Who we are, so we tell them
We are the Blackbirds, mighty mighty Blackbirds. ∎

The Staff

Edwin Graham Carpenter was a dairy farmer from Pennsylvania who moved to the South Carolina town of Moncks Corner in the 1920s. There he managed the dairy operation at the Gippy Plantation owned by Nicholas Roosevelt. Carpenter was hired in 1930 by J. Peter Grace to run Walworth Plantation in Eutawville, so he and wife Anne moved there and began a family. Chris was born in 1930 and George in 1933.

Chris developed an early love for horses, hunting and football, and he learned from working for his dad on the dairy farm the principle of attention to detail and the art of doing things right. "Never do anything half-baked," Edwin told his son.

Chris went to Sewanee Military Academy in Tennessee, played blocking back on the football team and was recruited by coach Red Sanders to play at Vanderbilt University. But after attending a University of North Carolina vs. Tennessee football game in Knoxville with a Sewanee teammate from Wadesboro, N.C., Carpenter had second thoughts about his college choice—particularly after Sanders left to become coach at Southern Cal.

"As a sixteen year old, I was enthralled with Charlie Justice and Carolina," Carpenter says. "That was the game he made his famous run and broke eleven tackles. The fans were singing, 'Tar Heel born, Tar Heel bred,' and I was taken with the whole thing. I just thought it was great."

Carpenter enrolled at Carolina in the fall of 1948 as a walk-on and played on the undefeated JV team. He was put on scholarship by coach Carl Snavely entering his sophomore season in 1949, and the plan was to red-shirt the fourth-team blocking back. Carpenter was in his

Chris Carpenter gets victory ride from David Parker (L) and Brent Milgrom following state semifinal win over Greensboro Page in 1963.

Bill Campbell (L-R), Danny Talbott, Chris Carpenter and Henry Trevathan at practice in 1961.

street clothes on the sidelines for the Tar Heels' second game of the year, in Kenan Stadium against Georgia, and his job was to chart the Tar Heels' offensive play calls. But after two blocking backs ahead of him on the depth chart left the game with injuries, Snavely told Carpenter to go put his uniform on. By the time he returned, the third-team blocking back had been knocked out and Carpenter was now in the game. He played the rest of the year and started in the Cotton Bowl against Rice on New Year's Day 1950.

Carpenter entered the reserves later that year and was called into active duty just before preseason camp opened in August 1950. He was stationed at Paris Island and played on the Marine Corps football team for two seasons before being released. He met several players from coach Jim Tatum's program at the University of Maryland during his Marine enlistment and actually had the opportunity to meet Tatum and discuss the idea of playing for the Terrapins upon his military release. At the urging of Tar Heel assistant coach Marvin Bass, however, Carpenter returned to Chapel Hill in January 1953. But a nagging knee injury and a different coaching style in new Tar Heel coach George Barclay prompted Carpenter to leave the program.

"Football just wasn't fun anymore," he says.

Carpenter graduated from Chapel Hill in January 1955 and soon moved north, thinking of a career in horse training and racing. By the end of the summer of 1956, however, Carpenter had begun rethinking that plan. "My mother didn't think it was a good idea," he says. He was driving back to South Carolina on Labor Day weekend and stopped in Chapel Hill to see Tatum, who had returned to his alma mater as head coach for the 1956 season after winning the national championship with the Terrapins in 1953 and finishing third in the Associated Press poll in 1955.

"So, what are you going to do?" Tatum asked.

"Coach, I really don't know," Carpenter answered.

"Well, I need a graduate assistant coach, someone to coach the freshman team," Tatum said. "The job is yours if you want it."

Carpenter liked the proposal and accepted. He earned his masters degree over the following year and got to witness Tatum's coaching gifts up close.

"Coach Snavely and coach Tatum were incredibly well-organized and detail oriented," Carpenter says. "I learned a lot from both of them. As a player under coach Snavely, you'd show up on Monday after a game and there'd be a letter in your box. It would have notes on the game, what you did right, what you did wrong, what you needed to work on that week. It might say, 'Good block on that play.' Or it might say, 'You're in Charlie's way … *get the hell out of Charlie's way!'* Coach Snavely was one of the first coaches to get into film study in a big way.

"Coach Tatum took all of that a step beyond. Sitting next to him in the meeting room, I marveled over how precise he was. He was also a great motivator. He had very few rules, but you had better master the ones he did have."

After collecting his master's degree in the summer of 1957, Carpenter was approached by Ken Yarborough, a teammate on the 1953 Tar Heel squad. Yarborough had just accepted the head coaching job at Rocky Mount Senior High and offered Carpenter a job as his assistant.

"I was single and just out of grad school," Carpenter says. "I thought it was a great idea."

Carpenter came to Rocky Mount and immediately was garnished with the nickname "Three Cs" or "Triple C"—for Coach Chris Carpenter.

Jim Horn (L) and Henry Trevathan at the film projector; Horn was an assistant to Chris Carpenter for the 1959 and 1960 seasons, Trevathan from 1959-63.

Yarborough left after one year to move to High Point and enter the textile industry. Carpenter was given some consideration for the head coaching job. But he was only twenty-eight years old, and the Rocky Mount administration and athletic director Bill Lundy thought him too young for the job. They hired Don Hipps, a former player at Wake Forest, and Hipps brought a fellow Demon Deacon named Jim Horn as an assistant coach. He asked Carpenter to stay on as a varsity assistant.

"I almost left," Carpenter says. "I was disappointed I wasn't named head coach. But they were right. I wasn't ready for the job. I figured I liked the town and I liked the school, so I might as well stay.

"It was a good decision. I learned a lot from Don Hipps. I didn't learn so much about Xs and Os, but about how to coach high school players, how to relate to them,

The 1964 "Hi-Noc-Ar" yearbook was dedicated to the Blackbird coaching staff (clockwise from lower right): Bill Lundy, Dudley Whitley, Chris Carpenter, Henry Trevathan, Don Stallings and Johnny Stott.

how to discipline them, how to develop a rapport with them."

Hipps' wife wasn't fond of Eastern North Carolina and, after the 1958 season, talked her husband into moving back to the western part of the state, and Hipps landed a job as an assistant at Garinger High in Charlotte. This time, Lundy and the school board thought Carpenter had grown and learned enough to take over the top job.

"Chris was now ready," says Henry Trevathan, the junior high coach. "He was absolutely ready.

"Chris had played under Carl Snavely, a great coach, and been a graduate assistant to Jim Tatum, also a great coach. Coaching under Tatum was like saying you'd coached under Bear Bryant or Joe Paterno. Tatum was as big as any of those names. Chris had been a good football player. He'd paid his dues at Rocky Mount and learned his craft of working with young kids."

Carpenter was also blessed with *it*—that undefined amalgam of leadership, intelligence and personal qualities that blend into the recipe for an outstanding head coach.

"He had that persona," Trevathan says. "A good coach is one who is strong enough to implant his own style, his own image on the program. He's not only knowledgeable and capable but has a strong image. By image, I mean personality, character, physical stature. Chris had the presence that drafted a lot of things in his wake. Chris led and the team and the town followed.

"Those qualities would have worked at the University of Tennessee or the Washington Redskins."

Carpenter started at $4,000 and worked two extra jobs in the summer to help make ends meet—teaching driver's education and managing the concessions operation at the minor-league baseball games. He married his girlfriend of two years in 1958, and Martha and Chris first lived in Sunset Apartments and then bought a house on Thomas Street when they started a family with three children—Ann, Sarah and Chris Jr.

Among Carpenter's first moves as head coach were to move Trevathan up from the junior high to assist with the varsity and ask Horn to stay on as an assistant. Horn would remain on staff for the 1959 and '60 seasons, and Trevathan was on the staff through the two state title teams in 1962 and '63 before leaving to build a juggernaut program at Wilson Fike High in 1964.

Trevathan grew up in Fountain and grew to love the game of football though he was smaller than most boys and never a standout player. He played at Virginia Episcopal School and then attended UNC with designs on becoming a doctor. By the age of twenty-two, however, Trevathan had dropped out of college and was selling ice

QB Jimmy Arrington (44) confers with Chris Carpenter and Don Stallings during 1963 game.

cream bars on the beach in Florida.

"I got to thinking about what I wanted to do with my life," he says. "It occurred to me how much I loved sports. I was a sports nut. I remembered playing football all day back in Fountain as a kid, and I thought coaching might be the answer for me."

Trevathan returned home, entered East Carolina Teachers College (later to become East Carolina University) and tried out for every sport possible in order to observe and learn how to coach. He took an eighteen-month break for Army service in the early 1950s, then graduated from college in 1955 and spent two years at Windsor High in Bertie County, coaching five sports and teaching five classes. He moved to Rocky Mount for the 1957 academic year to coach and teach at the junior high, and he got to know Carpenter and Horn well.

"We spent a lot of time talking about scheme and technique," Trevathan says. "The senior high coaches came over and helped me coach the junior high. We were starting to build a staff, we were starting to build some feeling of community."

Two years later, Horn left and Carpenter made another astute personnel move.

Don Stallings' father sold fuel oil, coal and wood. As a boy, Stallings was forever caked in the dust he picked up playing barefoot in the coal yard. One of the older boys in

Baseball coach Dudley Whitley considers his next move during Blackbirds' run to 1963 state title.

town told him, "You look like you've been wallowing in a coal bucket," and the nickname "Coal Bucket" stuck with Stallings from the age of twelve onward. If you ask an old-timer around Rocky Mount today if they know Don Stallings, they're likely to respond, "You mean Coal Bucket?"

Stallings was a standout on the Blackbird team that went 8-1-1 in 1955 and then was in Tatum's first recruiting class at Carolina. Carpenter was the freshman coach when Stallings arrived in Chapel Hill in 1956, and he remembers Stallings as a "big, bubbly guy, the kind you meet and take an immediate liking to." Stallings lettered three years as an offensive lineman and then was drafted in the fifth round by the Washington Redskins. He played one year of professional ball, but since the money was nothing special in pro ball at the time ($11,000 a year), Stallings left to come home in the summer of 1961 and help his ailing father in the family business. He came to see Carpenter and watch the Blackbirds practice in August that year.

One day, Carpenter said, "Bucket, why don't you help us out coaching? We don't have enough people."

Stallings agreed and spent the next four years as a volunteer assistant coach.

"He was a local hero, local guy made good," says David Parker, a two-way lineman on the 1962 and '63 teams. "He had huge credibility with the kids. He would always be in your face, telling you to be tough. He had a big, tough presence, but there was a gentle side to him as well. He made a lot of difference. We were a better team because of Coal Bucket."

Another lineman who benefited from Stallings' coaching was Steve Wright.

"I was in awe of Don," says Wright, a senior guard on the 1962 state title team. "He was the biggest man I'd ever seen and he could still out-run me. He brought a lot of plays from the Redskins, a lot of finesse plays. We weren't big enough to overpower people, to just run up the middle. We used a lot of bootlegs and traps."

The final component of the coaching staff for the glory days run was Dudley Whitley, a native of Rocky Mount who brought a chipper personality and profound love of baseball to the staff.

Whitley graduated from Rocky Mount in 1952 and played all three sports. He excelled at baseball and went to N.C. State, where he played for four years. He graduated in 1956 and played four years in the Milwaukee Braves organization. Whitley took a job as a physical education teacher and football, basketball and baseball coach at R.M. Wilson Junior High for the 1959-60 school year when Trevathan vacated those roles to move to the Senior High.

"I was at the junior high, but I felt very much a part of the high school program," Whitley says. "Chris said he wanted the junior high doing what the high school was doing. There was a lot of cohesiveness between the junior and senior high schools. The high school coaches came to see us practice and play games. They knew our personnel and who was coming along for the future."

Whitley's job was to scout the opposition on Friday nights, and he traveled across Eastern North Carolina to preview the teams run by coaches like Leon Brogden in Wilmington, Buddy Luper in Fayetteville and Clyde Walker in Raleigh. Whitley diagrammed plays as the game evolved and dictated notes and observations into a tape recorder. After a few hours sleep after getting back to Rocky Mount, Whitley was up early on Saturday morning to transcribe his notes and prepare the scouting report for Carpenter, Trevathan and Stallings to use in putting their game plan together.

"Dudley Whitley was a man who truly found his calling—leading young people and being around athletics," Trevathan says. "He was in the right business. His exuberance and enthusiasm were right out front. Young people fell right in line behind him. It was almost like he was one of them."

Meanwhile, Bill Lundy provided guidance to the younger football coaches and ran the department with a close eye to the bottom line, all the while coaching the basketball team and tennis teams to consistent levels of success.

Lundy was born in 1915 and grew up in the east Tennessee town of Erwin, a railroad community that would provide a level of attraction to moving to Rocky Mount as a young adult. He loved basketball and tennis as a youth and, after graduating from East Tennessee State University, spent four years in the Navy. He married his high school sweetheart and then coached basketball for one year at Monticello College in Arkansas. A friend and mentor had worked for the local YMCA and encouraged Lundy to look into a career in YMCA administration. There were two openings in 1945 for directors, one in Spartanburg, Tenn., and the other in Rocky Mount. He interviewed for and was offered the job in Rocky Mount, and he moved there in 1946, with his bride, Thelma, following one year later.

"Rocky Mount had a good feel to it," says Thelma, who still lives there. "It was a railroad town and it was familiar to us. Bill got into the YMCA work, and he enjoyed teaching and working with young people. But raising money and keeping the building up were distractions from what he really enjoyed doing."

Lundy left the YMCA in 1949 to join the staff at Rocky Mount High as basketball and tennis coach. He moved

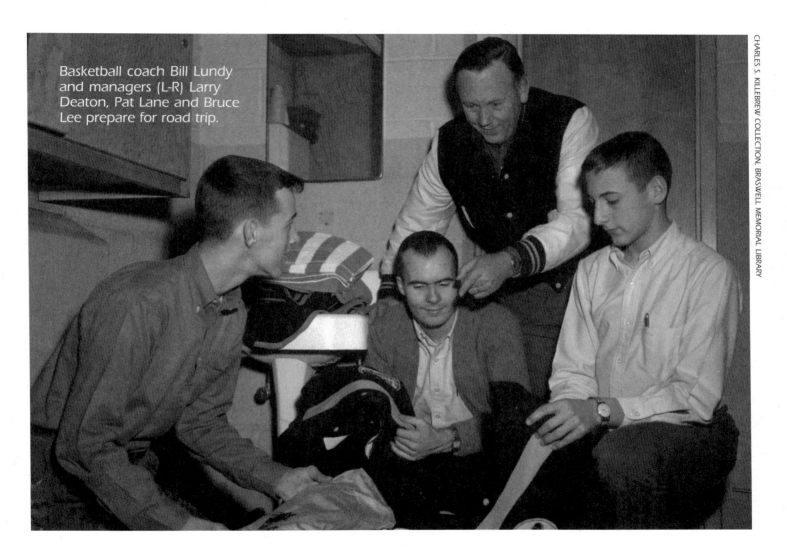
Basketball coach Bill Lundy and managers (L-R) Larry Deaton, Pat Lane and Bruce Lee prepare for road trip.

into the athletic director role when long-time football coach and athletic director E.E. "Knocker" Adkins resigned in 1955.

Lundy was forty-four and Carpenter twenty-nine when Carpenter took the head football job in 1959. Carpenter says Lundy was like a "second father to me," and Lundy's sons, Mike and Jerry, played ball for Carpenter.

"He kept me from doing silly things," Carpenter says.

Lundy originally told Carpenter he had to coach two sports, so his second one was JV basketball.

"I got two technicals the first game and three the second game," Carpenter says. "That was the end of my basketball coaching career. Bill moved me to golf. That wasn't a bad deal. Palmer Maples was the pro at Benvenue Country Club, and all the football coaches in the area were the golf coaches as well. We'd play our matches while the kids were playing their's."

Lundy maintained a tight hand on the athletic department coffers, despite the fact the team's improving fortunes on the football field kept a steady stream of revenue coming in from gate and concession receipts.

"I used to cuss coach Lundy all the time because he'd not give me any money for this or that," Carpenter says. "I'd want to buy a piece of equipment, a blocking sled or something, but he'd say he didn't have the money. I had to get someone to donate the money. I do know this: The athletic department was in the black after our second year. Coach Lundy did not have to worry about paying for Rocky Mount athletics. It was all done on gate receipts and contributions. We didn't get a nickel from the state."

The coaches worked well together and the chemistry was excellent. The 1964 *Hi-Noc-Ar* yearbook was dedicated to the staff, noting "The ease with which they work together has paid off in a unified athletic program at Senior High and a string of state championships." The coaches walked a fine line between running a tight ship with their players while maintaining a semblance of light-heartedness. "They seem to go at it like kids in a sandlot baseball game," the yearbook's editors observed.

The coaches were fair game for the occasional practical joke. Carpenter took pride in the condition of the football practice field and pulled players out of study halls and gym classes to help rake and seed the field each spring. He was going to particular maintenance extremes during the spring of 1963 to insure the field would be in perfect shape for the coming August. A couple of players took the opportunity to plant some hybrid corn seed in the field.

"That corn jumped up like giant bean stalks when it got hot that summer," says Brent Milgrom, a rising senior at the time who went by the nickname "Plowboy." "Coach never accused me of being the culprit. But with me being from the farming community of Battleboro, I think he had a good idea."

But Carpenter also had strict rules, one of them being absolutely no drinking. He learned of a late-night party after a home football during the 1960 season and had to banish three players from the team.

"They were all starters, good football players," he says. "I hated to do it. But that was the rule."

The dreaded "fifteen-minute squad" was punishment for other infractions, such as being late for team meetings or getting caught smoking. Players went through a myriad of sprints, crab drills and up-downs after practice.

"I would not tolerate being late," Carpenter says. "First infraction, you were on the fifteen-minute squad. Second infraction, you could stay home and mow the grass. We did all kinds of fine exercises on the fifteen-minute squad. That was not a place you wanted to be."

"The coaches were our friends," Danny Talbott says. "Don't get me wrong, they would chew you out big-time. There's nothing left of my butt today because they chewed it all off. But we had coaches who cared about us as people, not only as athletes. They demanded we become the caliber of person we needed to be. We were well-trained, well-coached and always well-prepared.

"We were taught you take as much pride in that classroom as you did the athletic field. We studied our football plays, but we were also going to make our grades. You'd better not mess up in the classroom. You would have somebody talking to you later that afternoon."

David Parker remembers that Carpenter had a "little bit of a gruff side, but he was a pussy cat at heart. He was always funny, wisecracking jokes with the players. All the players viewed him as being very fair."

Parker and fellow lineman John Alexander were straight-A students and often the butt of Carpenter's jabs that the Blackbirds were saddled with "geniuses who can't block a lick" and hit "like Molly Putz."

"We were never allowed to think we were bigger than the game or better than anyone else," Talbott says. "There was not a lot of rah-rah. You did what you were

Dudley Whitley, Henry Trevathan on sidelines in Junior High game.

Blackbirds Digit Laughridge (33) and Billy Warren and cheerleaders (L-R) Ginger Ryals and Carol Mortimer rejoice with Chris Carpenter following 26-6 win at Wilmington in 1963.

expected to do. You went out there to win. We were taught to play hard and taught to win."

One instance Parker cites of Carpenter's sense of fairness occurred during August 1963, when Parker entered his senior season in the best physical shape of his life. Parker, a guard, was put into a group with the backs and ends for the requisite mile run. Backs and ends had to beat six minutes in the mile to prove they had followed the off-season conditioning regimen. If they missed, there was the devil to pay in the form of crab drills and grass drills after practice.

"Here I was, a lineman at 5-11, 180 pounds, running with the backs," Parker says. "After three laps, I was in front and everyone was cheering me on. Then I hit a wall, fell out and flaked out in the grass, throwing up all over the place. All the coaches knew what I had done was stupid, out there trying to outrun the backs. But Chris knew I was in shape. So he didn't put me in the grass drills. I loved him for being fair in that respect."

Doubie Snow, captain of the 1959 team and later a scholarship player at N.C. State University, remembers running wind sprints after practice during his senior season. As Carpenter kept sending the players through sprint after sprint after sprint, Snow was bent over, sucking for air and said, "You son of a bitch."

Carpenter heard something and certainly caught the last word. He blew his whistle and yelled, "Who said that?"

Snow raised his hand and said, "I did, Coach."

"What did you say, Snow?" Carpenter asked.

"I said, 'I'm just as tired as a son of a bitch,'" Snow answered.

"That'll be five laps for you after practice," Carpenter responded.

Carpenter had a good feel for team psychology. The Blackbirds were hosting Greensboro Page in the semifinals of the 1963 playoffs, and Carpenter addressed the team pre-game in the school lounge before the players walked to the stadium. His message was to the effect that the team had accomplished more than anyone could have hoped for, given the departure of All-State quarterback Danny Talbott and several other key players. He told the Blackbirds to relax, that there was no pressure to exceed any expectations. His voice was calm and casual.

"I remember exchanging glances with several of my teammates, all of us sharing the expression, 'Can you believe old Triple C is saying this?'" says Parker. "Where was the 'put a helmet under their chin' or 'give them a huge forearm on the first play and make them want to quit' kind of stuff?"

The result: Rocky Mount 42, Page 0.

"The soft-sell worked perfectly," Parker says. "It relaxed everyone and put us at ease. We clicked in every phase of the game and pounded them all night. I've met several of the Page players living in Greensboro over the years and they never fail to mention how well Rocky Mount played that night."

Stallings remembers another game when the Blackbirds played lethargically in the first half, and as the coaches convened outside the locker room at halftime, Stallings said, "We've got to do something to psyche these kids up."

Carpenter considered the issue for a few seconds, then walked into the locker room.

"You guys stunk," he said. "You were awful."

Then he left the room, leaving the players to stew in their own juices and figure their problems out.

"We stood outside listening to them," Stallings says. "Whatever the problem was, they figured it out and we played well in the second half."

Carpenter's first team as head coach in 1959 notched a 7-2-1 mark and won the Eastern 4-A Conference (Rocky Mount's first league title in nineteen years) before losing to Garinger and All-State quarterback Gary Black 13-6 in the first round of the playoffs. In an interesting twist of fate, the Blackbirds met up with their former coach in that game: Don Hipps was now an assistant at Garinger.

"He knew everything we were doing and all the strengths and weaknesses of our players," Carpenter says. "He knew, for example, how fast Ronnie Jackson was and that you cannot let him get outside. Ronnie could fly. I was a young coach and made a critical mistake that game. I should have known that Don would keep Ronnie off the corners. If we'd gone with traps up the middle, Ronnie would be running still. I think of that often. A rookie mistake I guess you'd say."

Carpenter remembers early in his tenure losing to Wilmington and ace quarterback Roman Gabriel and the post-game exchange with Wildcats coach Leon Brogden. They shook hands and Brogden, the long-time New Hanover coach, congratulated Carpenter on the team's progress and encouraged him to keep working hard.

"He had this habit of pinching you on the back while he talked to you," Carpenter says. "I decided then and there I never wanted to lose to him again. I couldn't stand that pinching."

The 1960 team was 5-5, and the 1961 team returned no starters from that squad, leaving modest expectations entering the season. But the Blackbirds raced to a 6-0 start while allowing only five touchdowns. They traveled to Wilmington and beat New Hanover 33-0 in late September, with Talbott passing for three touchdowns to Billy Warren. The squad became known as the "team that shouldn't be but is." Lundy hung out a sign saying,

Joyous Blackbirds surround Chris Carpenter in locker room following 13-0 win at Goldsboro in 1963.

"Wanted: 6,000 Blackbird Fans" before a home game against Fayetteville in early October.

"This Rocky Mount team continues to amaze us," a Fayetteville scout said. "We look down the roster and see only a few names we were familiar with last year. A team with that much inexperience just isn't supposed to win like this one is doing."

Durham and Rocky Mount tied at 14-14 in week seven. After whipping Tarboro 33-7, the Blackbirds traveled to Charlotte's Myers Park, where they won 21-18. The regular season concluded with a 21-0 loss to Raleigh Broughton, but since it was the Eastern 4-A Conference's turn to get two teams into the four-team state playoffs, the Blackbirds would join Broughton in extending their seasons. For the second time in three years, Rocky Mount traveled to Garinger High in Charlotte for a playoff game.

Garinger led 7-0 just before halftime when Garinger recovered a Blackbird fumble and had the ball inside the ten. Garinger caught Rocky Mount off guard because one of the officials was standing over the ball before it had been snapped, and the Blackbirds didn't believe the ball was ready for play. But the center snapped it to the quarterback, who raced in for the score. Garinger took a 14-0 lead into halftime and had seized the momentum en route to a 21-0 victory. Carpenter protested the touchdown but to no avail.

"I confronted the official after the game about that play," Carpenter says. "He said, 'Well, it didn't matter. You got beat.' Needless to say, that official never again worked a game I coached."

Rocky Mount finished the season with an 8-2-1 record. The Blackbirds were now ready to overcome officials calls, bad breaks and injuries to field a championship team. The process was working.

"While all of this is going on, Bill Lundy believes in what he's doing as the athletic director," Trevathan says. "Chris Carpenter believes in what he's doing with the football program. They are rubbing elbows with the best, teams like Myers Park. The players are sensing they are good. Things are building up like kindling. And all along, we're watching what is coming along through the ranks. We've seen them since the fifth and sixth grade. We knew what we had coming along was every bit as good.

"And then you have Danny Talbott. Once in a while, nature comes along and gives us something special. And Danny was special." ■

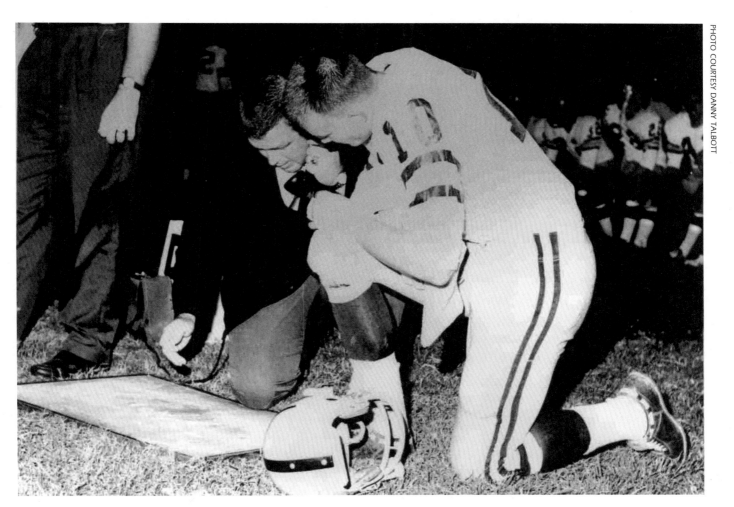
Chris Carpenter and Danny Talbott get input from Dudley Whitley over the phone on sidelines in 1962.

The Star

It was a big day in 1954 in Battleboro, a town about seven miles north of Rocky Mount, when the local midget league all-stars hosted a basketball tournament to christen the school's new auditorium and gymnasium. Country boys always seemed to grow and mature sooner than their in-town brethren, and the Battleboro players preened in their new uniforms, supplied by St. John's Episcopal Church, and bristled with confidence.

"Some of our ten and eleven year olds even had hair on their chests," remembers Brent Milgrom, whose father operated a peanut farm just outside of Battleboro. "We had one kid named Billy Dean Bullock. He was a *man* at ten years old. I don't know why, but the boys in the rural areas were very masculine at a younger age."

Milgrom, Bullock and their teammates watched with interest as the players from Northside Baptist Church in Rocky Mount disembarked their bus outside the school for their game.

"We were not very impressed," Milgrom says. "We were comfortable we'd beat them. Those city boys weren't coming out to our place and beating us."

Both teams started their pre-game warm-ups, with all the boys save one shooting the ball in the style of the day, the set-shot or push-shot, and in the case of the better players, the one-hand push shot popularized by Wake Forest's Dickie Hemric and the teachings of coach Everett Case at N.C. State University.

One of the Northside players, however, got the attention of the Battleboro team with his ability to shoot jump shots. *No one* at that level wielded the jump shot.

Danny Talbott even went beyond the top of the key

Danny Talbott drives for layup against Fayetteville during 1963 run to conference and state titles.

Talbott eludes a Goldsboro defender during 14-12 win in 1962; Blackbird Billy Warren throws a block.

and was knocking down jumpers.

"He was strong enough and coordinated enough to do things no one else could do," Milgrom says. "Billy Dean and I looked at one another and said, 'We're in trouble.'"

Milgrom can't remember the score of the game but is confident Northside won. And he clearly recalls the impression Talbott left on the town of Battleboro.

"He was special, there was no question," Milgrom says. "He brought the ball up the court and was as big and strong and talented as the front-court guys. He could drive and score at will. But he didn't do any fancy stuff. He never lost control of the ball, no matter how fast or slow he went. He was so capable and coordinated and far above anyone else on the floor."

The town of Rocky Mount and its opponents in football, basketball and baseball grew over the next decade to never be surprised at anything Talbott accomplished. He zig-zagged across the football field for touchdowns, played safety, punted and kicked extra points. He hit last-minute shots to lift the Blackbirds to numerous basketball victories. He hit better than .400 on the baseball field, pitched and played third base and once even retired East Mecklenburg while pitching with a broken hand.

"We had good coaching, a helluva group of athletes, and then Danny Talbott made the difference," says David Lamm, Rocky Mount Senior High Class of 1963. "If you needed a late shot, a late hit, a big play late in the game, Danny would make it. He was the Frank Merriwell type."

Adds Marion Barnes, a fellow senior with Talbott on the 1962 state champion football team: "You knew who the stars were and who the supporting cast was. Danny was a star. He could change things on the football field, the basketball court, the baseball field. He could do things no one else could do."

Talbott was the son of Joe and Lena Mae and brother of Robert and grew up in the mill section of Rocky Mount, just a couple of blocks east of Falls Road. Joe Talbott preached at a country church and also was a supervisor for Pepsi Cola Bottling Co. There was a softball field in the neighborhood owned and maintained by Rocky Mount Mills, and Talbott remembers having a ball of some kind in his hand from the age of three. And it never mattered what kind of ball it was—he simply went with the seasons.

"It was our way of life," Talbott says. "After the football season, we'd put away our cleats and begin basketball. As soon as that ended, we'd go on to baseball."

Bernie Capps' father owned a grocery store just a few blocks from the Talbott home, and Capps was a manager on the early 1960s football teams at Rocky Mount Senior High. He went into education and today is on the faculty and athletic training staff at the high school.

Celebrating the 1963 state basketball title were (L-R): Rocky Mount Schools Superintendent D.S. Johnson, Mayor Billy Harrison, Principal C.J. Edson, Danny Talbott and Athletic Director Bill Lundy.

"Today there is much more specialization," Capps says. "Back then they played football, basketball and baseball. I try to tell our kids now to play everything they can. If you have God-given ability, don't waste it on one sport, play as many as you can play. I think it helps all the athletic programs."

An early growth spurt gave Talbott several extra inches of height than most boys his age. Lamm's mother dug out a photo from a youth league baseball team that shows Talbott's arm pits at the level of the other players' heads. Mike Lundy, son of Blackbird basketball coach Bill Lundy, remembers Talbott being a force in sandlot games against players four or five years older. "Danny just acted older than his age," Lundy says. "He had a presence at an early age."

The City Recreation League had a rule for its basketball games that if a player scored twenty points, he had to come out for the rest of the game.

"Danny would score as many as he wanted to," says Bob Williams, a youth league coach and sports editor of the *Rocky Mount Telegram*. "If they were playing someone who managed to keep the game close, Danny would get his eighteen points, then stay in the game to pass and rebound."

Chris Carpenter and Henry Trevathan watched Talbott evolve through the late 1950s.

"We could see we had some good players coming along in junior high," says Carpenter. "Henry and I would go to Little League games and watch Danny. You could tell he was something special at an early age. Whichever team he was on was going to win, period. He could kick it better than our guys on the varsity."

Years later, Trevathan put together an exhaustive statistical recap of Talbott's career in preparing his nomination for the North Carolina Sports Hall of Fame.

"I went through every game he played," Trevathan says. "I got to re-live it. I'd lived it once and then did it a second time. When you do it the second time, certain things pop out that you missed the first time. The second time was even greater."

Talbott's first basketball game came as a sophomore against Kinston, a perennial Eastern North Carolina power. He scored twenty points and had twenty rebounds.

"Was he coached to do that?" Trevathan muses. "You read through every game for three years of football, basketball and baseball, and you see that coaching was a minor part of it. A cliché in the coaching business is to know what *not* to coach. Danny required less coaching than anyone you'd ever seen."

The annals of Blackbird athletics are full of the exploits of the six-foot, 180-pound athlete. One of the most oft-cited was his forty-three yard run for the game-winning touchdown against Raleigh Broughton to clinch the 1962 Eastern 4-A Conference title.

"I think everybody on that team had a shot at him and some of them twice," says Bill Warren, who joined Talbott in the starting lineups of all three state title teams in 1962-63. "And he was just very good at weaving and shifting and able to do a 'Choo Choo' Justice type run. He had that kind of movement. He was able to stop and go in one direction. He had great spin moves. He was just a phenomenal player."

David Parker was a guard and remembers never blocking anyone on the play but following Talbott down the field.

"He just kept reversing field, back and forth," Parker says. "It was a phenomenal play. He must have run through everyone twice. I was exhausted and he was looking faster and better and more elusive than anyone on the field."

"Watching the film of that play was awesome," adds guard Steve Wright. "Everyone threw a block, knocked someone down, got up to see where Danny was and then looked for someone else to block."

Trevathan marvels at Talbott's patience and gamesmanship and wonders if either had a role in that late-game run against Broughton.

"I've talked to various opponents over the years, and they were amazed at how Danny talked to them during the game," Trevathan says. "He'd pat them on the rump, tell them 'Nice play.' All of a sudden, they're saying, 'Hey, Danny talked to me, he's a good guy, we're having fun.'

"What they didn't know was that with that interaction, Danny might be getting you to ease up a little bit. Deep down inside, he was figuring out how to beat you. When Danny was talking to you and making you feel good about everything, you should have seen he was pulling deeper and deeper within himself. The hammer was going to drop."

And it wasn't pure fleetness of foot that allowed Talbott to gain so many yards.

"He was not all that fast," says Eddie Baysden, who followed Talbott by three years in high school and today is executive director of the Rocky Mount Area Chamber of Commerce. "But if you were going to go *here*, he'd know it and go *there*. He was uncanny knowing where you were going. He was a darter. He could lull you to sleep and then dart past you in the blink of an eye."

Carpenter had no qualms about turning the wheel over to Talbott to manage the offense.

"Talbott was unbelievably savvy about things," Carpenter says. "He knew exactly what play to run at any given time. The players absolutely trusted him. It

Sophomore Talbott (L), senior Gus Tulloss show punting form prior to 1960 football season.

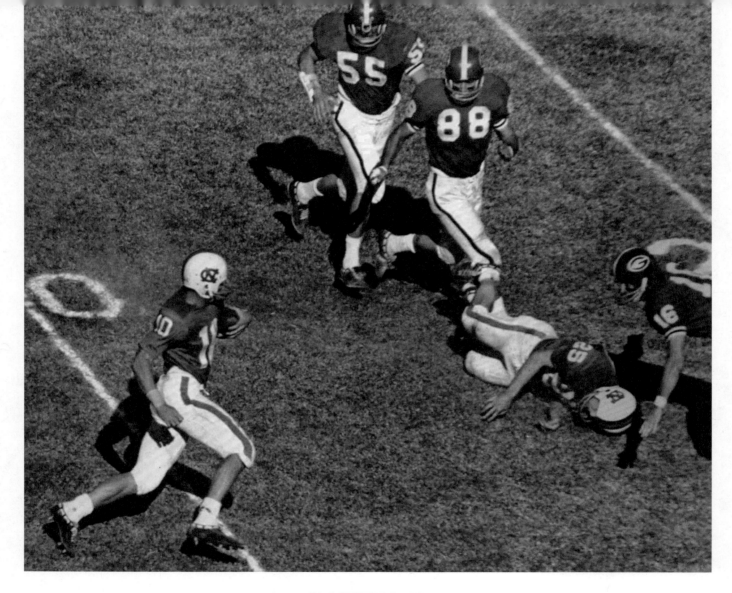

BLACKBIRDS 78

Talbott poses with UNC coach Jim Hickey (above left) in his living room in the spring of 1963 after signing to play for the Tar Heels. Talbott led the Atlantic Coast Conference in total offense in 1965 and gained 18 yards on this run against Georgia (left). He was first team All-ACC for three straight years in baseball.

amazes me today the lack of input quarterbacks have in calling their own plays. Everything's called by the coach in the booth. But no one had a better feel for what was going on than Danny."

Marion Barnes remembers Talbott essentially drawing up plays in the dirt as games evolved as he got a feel for what the opposition could or could not do.

"Danny would say, 'If you'll block this guy and you'll block this guy, and you run this route, I promise I'll get you the ball.' And he'd do exactly what he said he'd do," Barnes says. "One night we were playing Henderson. Danny looked at me and said, 'You block this guy on the end, and I'll run it all the way back.' And he did. Problem was, I got called for clipping."

Despite all the notoriety, Talbott was popular with his teammates, never got a big head and worked to elevate the performance levels of those around him.

"Some say the worst thing that can happen is to have that star," Trevathan says. "There've been a lot of stars that ruined you. 'If I could get rid of that *star*, I could have a good team.' Barry Bonds comes to mind. One rotten apple and all that. But Danny was a good kid. He was humble and level-headed."

"Danny made the kids around him better players, and they didn't resent that," says Dudley Whitley, the Blackbirds' head baseball coach and an assistant football coach. "They appreciated his talents. They fed off his ability. They were able to raise the level of their own game. They looked at him to make a big play at the right time. Then they began to say, 'Maybe I can make that play.'"

Long-time New Hanover High coach Leon Brogden said Talbott was "the best high school athlete I ever saw," and colleges around the nation clamored for his services during his senior year in 1962-63. Talbott considered all the major ACC schools in North Carolina and took a recruiting visit to Tennessee as well and eventually signed with the University of North Carolina. He played all three sports on the Tar Heel JV teams (this a decade before freshman eligibility), then gave up basketball after his freshman year, believing he could play the game at the major-college level but probably not beyond that.

Talbott was the starting quarterback as a sophomore in 1964 and helped the Tar Heels upset Michigan State 21-15 in Kenan Stadium in the second game of the year. But he suffered bruised ribs against LSU two weeks later and was less than a hundred percent the rest of the year.

Tar Heel coach Jim Hickey installed a spread offense in 1965 to showcase Talbott's abilities. Carolina lost at home to Michigan 31-24 in the season opener, then traveled to Ohio State. Talbott was 11-of-16 for 127 yards in leading Carolina to a 14-3 upset.

"That was a phenomenal experience, silencing that

many fans," Talbott said of the Buckeye crowd of more than 80,000.

The Tar Heels had a Jekyll-and-Hyde personality that year, playing the powerhouses tough and losing their focus against lesser teams. They followed the big win in Columbus by losing at home to lowly Virginia and finished the year with a 4-6 record. Still, Talbott led the ACC with 1,477 yards total offense and was named player of the year.

Talbott was mentioned as a Heisman Trophy candidate entering the 1966 season, and the year was off to a rousing start with a 21-7 upset win over Michigan in Ann Arbor in the third game of the year. Talbott suffered a badly sprained ankle the following week at Notre Dame and was never full speed the rest of his senior year. Carolina slumped to 2-8 and Hickey resigned to become athletic director at the University of Connecticut.

"If he'd had a supporting cast, there's no telling what he'd have done," says Barnes, a Tar Heel letterman in 1966. "He could have won the Heisman Trophy. He could play in the big-time. But he was always hurt. He never had any protection. He had a lack of support on both sides of the ball. We might have had one or two good players, but not enough of them."

Talbott made first-team All-ACC three years running in baseball, finishing with a career batting average of .357 and leading Carolina to the '66 College World Series.

He was drafted by the NFL's San Francisco 49ers in the 1967 draft but instead opted for pro baseball. He played one year of minor league ball—with the Baltimore Orioles' farm team in Miami—then decided to give football a try when his rights were acquired by the Washington Redskins. He spent three years backing up Sonny Jurgenson and Frank Ryan and "carrying Vince Lombardi's clipboard."

Talbott then returned home and enjoyed a successful career of thirty-three years in pharmaceutical sales, retiring in early 2007. Over the years, he learned to play tennis and became an accomplished player.

"Danny was just something special, he could do anything," Warren says. "He picked up tennis and before long was serving with one hand and hitting ground strokes with the other. He was absolutely the best all-around athlete I'd ever seen in doing everything."

Talbott doesn't play much tennis any longer and now directs most of his sporting hours to the fickle arena of golf. "It's the hardest game I've ever tried," he says. "That sucker is just sitting there, daring you to hit it. It's a challenge, but it's a lot of fun."

Odds are that Danny Talbott, an eight to eleven-handicap on the golf course, will master that game in time as well. ∎

The Edges

Among the elements that made Rocky Mount's football teams special in the early to mid-1960s were the game plans, film study and advanced schematic approach head coach Chris Carpenter brought to the program after his football educations under Carl Snavely and Jim Tatum at the University of North Carolina.

And the fact that his players were smart enough to grasp the concepts and execute them in competition.

"What set those teams apart were the kids' intellects," says Don Stallings, a former Blackbird player who was a volunteer assistant coach under Carpenter. "Look at what they've gone on to do—doctors, lawyers, every profession imaginable. We could make changes on the fly, at halftime, between series. We'd put in new game plans week-to-week—install four or five new plays for a particular team. That was not the norm for high school teams at the time."

"We were very fortunate," adds Dudley Whitley, the coach at R.M. Wilson Junior High and a varsity assistant coach. "Not only were they good athletes, but they were good kids and they were smart. They bought into the grading system that Chris implemented. It was important to them that they did well and got good grades for their performances. We had bright youngsters who understood what we had to do."

Of course, not everyone was razor-sharp upstairs. Carpenter chuckles thinking of one lineman who couldn't consistently tell his left from his right. Assistant coach Henry Trevathan tied a red ribbon on the kid's left shoe to help him keep remember one direction from the other.

"There was a high degree of confidence in the coach-

Chris Carpenter at the chalkboard with end Billy Warren (C) and guard David Parker.

ing staff that if you followed their scheme or game plan each week, we'd be successful," says David Parker, a starting lineman on the 1962-63 state 4-A title squads.

"Our coaches were doing things back then not everyone in high school was doing, like watching film," adds Billy Warren, a starting end both of those seasons. "We were the best-prepared team out there. We may not have had the best talent, but we were the best-prepared team week in and week out."

Film for each game was dispatched by bus immediately after the contest on Friday night to the processing lab in Greenville, and a Blackbird team manager would pick it up Saturday night at the bus station. The coaches graded the film Sunday afternoon after dinner, assessing each player a letter grade in time for a team meeting at 5 p.m. The team watched the film together, then broke into position meetings. By that time, the managers had picked up the film from the next opponent, with the schools swapping their two most recent games. The coaches would break for Hardees hamburgers and then study the opponent's film until late in the night.

"I was a great believer in film study," Carpenter says. "I convinced everyone else early on. I was a firm believer that you could not know what somebody was doing unless you looked at him on film."

One year Carpenter talked athletic director Bill Lundy into paying for film and processing of junior high games. He used the footage to show Trevathan that his opinion of one particular player was a little off the mark.

"Henry thought this kid was the greatest thing since sliced bread," Carpenter says. "He said, 'You're going to love this one.' Well, we watched the film and this kid Henry thought was so good didn't block anybody and didn't tackle anybody. He was an escape artist on both sides of the ball."

Carpenter was a staunch believer in letting his quarterback on offense and middle linebacker on defense make all the play calls.

"We did not signal anything from the sidelines," Carpenter says. "You can't see anything from the sidelines. I sure can't see where players are lined up—head-up, shaded inside, whatever. I believed you get a smart kid in your key positions and turn it over to him."

Carpenter remembers a game against Fayetteville in 1964 when linebacker Don Rabon called what Carpenter termed "the finest defensive game I've ever seen."

"Don recognized their sets and tendencies," Carpenter says of Rabon, who later went to Appalachian State University on a football scholarship. "He had us where we were supposed to be every single play. Fayetteville had a couple of backs that were out of sight. Don knew what they were going to run and he'd call the defense

The 1962 offense: Along the line (L-R) are Dennis Newell, Bobby Jones, Butch Clayton, Wayne Bulluck, Steve Wright, John Alexander and Billy Warren. Danny Talbott is the quarterback and is flanked by Digit Laughridge, Wayne Daughtridge and Wrennie Pitt.

we'd set up during the week. Every time they did something, we were there."

Thirty years after his playing career ended, quarterback Danny Talbott bristles at the control-freak attributes of nearly all coaches in modern football. Talbott knew the game plan and was given total freedom to call the plays.

"It irritates me to death today in football where the quarterbacks never get to call their own plays," Talbott says. "I always felt I was smart enough as a quarterback to get us in the right play. I would listen to what the guys had to say. A receiver might come up and say, 'Danny, that cornerback's leaning one way. I think we can go the other way and hit a big one.'"

Talbott was comfortable making suggestions to the coaches, who in turn were secure enough to listen and evaluate the ideas. During the bus ride to Winston-Salem for the 1962 state championship game against Winston-Salem Reynolds, Talbott had an idea and made his way to the front of the bus, where Carpenter was sitting.

"Coach, I was thinking about something," Talbott said. "We haven't run the shotgun much all year. What if we open in the shotgun and catch them by surprise?"

Carpenter agreed it was a good idea, and the Blackbirds came out early in the shotgun. They took the opening kick-off and scored quickly, with Talbott hitting end Bob Sides with a forty-yard pass for the opening score in a 21-6 victory.

"Chris was able to turn that loose," Talbott says. "Some coaches have a hard time doing that, not having their finger on every little thing. He allowed the kids to assume some responsibility for what they were doing."

That's not to say that Carpenter and his coaches didn't make tweaks and adjustments as the game evolved.

"Chris was one of the best strategists I've ever seen," Marion Barnes says. "He was great at making on-field adjustments. He'd watch one or two series and know what to do. He'd say, 'They're a little quicker than I thought. Let's change to this, let's do that.'"

Rocky Mount's two state championship seasons were built around defense. The Blackbirds allowed only sixty-nine points in 1962 (an average of less than six points a game), and the 1963 defense was even stingier with a points-allowed total of fifty-one. During the second half of the 1963 regular season, they allowed only two touchdowns. They had ten shutouts over the two seasons. The 1963 team allowed Myer's Park two first downs, and

HOW MANY MORE?

Betty Armstrong's cartoon counted the Blackbirds' victims during the fall of 1962.

Kinston completed just one pass for three yards.

The Blackbirds played a 5-3 alignment up front, a scheme Carpenter got from Rockingham High coach Bill Eustler at the 1961 East-West Game in Greensboro. They slanted the nose guard and two tackles, and the linebackers had reads on the backs and ends and reacted accordingly. They played zone in secondary, as Carpenter preferred to have a "centerfielder" to cover deep and never allow the long ball, albeit being prone to underneath passes on occasion.

"You had to have smart linebackers," Carpenter says. "That was the key. Depending on the reads, you might have six players go to the same spot. They'd not have enough people to block you. Other times, you'd be slanting your linemen to one side but the linebackers' reads would have them go somewhere else if they were running some misdirection stuff. We'd be sitting on them waiting. But you had to have bright kids who could do that."

On offense, the Blackbirds ran the split-T, an attack Carpenter learned under Tatum at Carolina. They also used some of Tatum's shotgun formation to take advantage of Talbott's skills.

"We could have done a lot more with the shotgun, but we had some pretty good running backs," Carpenter says, referring to players like halfbacks Wrennie Pitt, Digit Laughridge and Darrell Johnson and fullback Wayne Daughtridge. "And we were never interested in scoring a bunch of points and running up the score. We were more interested in making sure you *didn't* score. And we knew Danny would get us enough points.

"We started using Danny's arm at the end of his sophomore season (1960). He could throw the ball well. We certainly used his kicking ability. We could have made it one-man team, but we had too many other kids you didn't want to deprive."

Carpenter remembers the challenge of playing coach Gus Purcell's Myers Park team in the first playoff game in 1962.

"They had a great, great passing attack," Carpenter says. "They slaughtered everyone. I said, 'Gentlemen, we cannot afford to give them the football. Tighten it up because when we get the football, we are keeping it.'"

The Blackbirds won the toss, elected to receive and began a clock-churning, ball-possession series of plays built around "56 run," an off-tackle play behind end Billy Warren and tackle John Alexander. The success of the play depended on Warren and Alexander working together at the line of scrimmage to make the proper blocking call, depending on what the defense was showing. One call would be to double-team the tackle and kick out with the fullback. Another would be an "X" move, with the end blocking down on the tackle, Alexander pulling behind him and kicking out the end, and the fullback running through and blocking the linebacker. The third call was "Wham," where the end turned out the defensive end, the tackle blocked the defensive tackle down, and the fullback would lead through the hole.

"Three times on fourth down I remember us running 56," Carpenter says. "Warren and Alexander would blow them off. We'd pick up the yards and keep moving the ball.

"You could do things with our kids. I don't know if other coaches could or could not, but they didn't seem to use much imagination. But we could do an awful lot with our kids because they were so smart."

One year on offense, Carpenter inserted the "lonesome end" formation to help get an edge, with end Ralph Williams never returning to the huddle between snaps and remaining positioned to one boundary or the other. The quarterback signaled the plays to him after breaking the huddle.

"We got the idea from Bill Murray and Duke," Carpenter says. "We couldn't throw the ball out of the backyard, but the defense couldn't assume that. They had to cover Ralph every snap, which made them change the configuration of their secondary. You know, I don't think we threw one pass to him all year."

Carpenter used Warren to bait Broughton into a key lapse during the 1963 regular-season finale. For the first three quarters, Warren was instructed to run out-patterns at three-quarter speed.

"I'm going to need you to run a post-pattern later the game," Carpenter said. "I'm going to need you to be faster than you've been, and it's going to be a big play."

In the fourth quarter, Carpenter pulled Warren aside and told him the time had come to set the trap. The game was tied at 0-0.

Carpenter, Bob Sides and Bobby Jones watch Blackbird highlights at Sportsman's Club meeting.

"The corner and safety will be looking for the out," Carpenter said. "Give them the fake and you'll have the middle all to yourself. We'll get the ball to you."

Jimmy Arrington hit Warren on a thirty-one yard pass to the nineteen. Two plays later, Laughridge scored from the three for the only score in a 6-0 victory.

Carpenter came to defensive end Brent Milgrom several games into the 1962 season with an idea for the kick-off cover unit. He wanted Milgrom to go in motion from one side or the other before the kick-off was made, then cut up field upon the kick. Return teams handle blocking assignments by designating Player A, for example, with blocking the first defender to the right of the kicker, Player B to the second man, etc. Since Milgrom's starting point varied with each kick, the return team could never get its blocking assignments correct, and Milgrom raced downfield unblocked all season and half of the next.

"To my knowledge, no one else was using a man in that fashion, a position today they call the 'gunner,'" Milgrom says. "Then some of the smarter teams began using a wedge for the ball carrier to make sure he had protection. That was even better, because I had a thirty-yard running start, and they were just standing there. What fun."

The defense held Myers Park four downs inside the one yard-line in state playoffs in Charlotte in 1962. When the offense came out, Talbott called for a quarterback sneak. Guard Steve Wright looked at the tackle beside him and suggested they improvise with a different blocking pattern. They agreed and told Talbott what was going to happen. The result was a fifteen-yard quarterback sneak that got the Blackbirds off the goal line on the way to a 21-6 victory.

"The next day watching film, the coaches jumped me for blocking the wrong guy," Wright says. "I said, 'No coach, we planned it that way.'"

Despite all the team's success with X-and-O machinations, it was the lack of a key strategic adjustment that haunts Carpenter to this day. The Blackbirds had effectively shut down the single wing offense of coach Red Wilson and Winston-Salem Reynolds in the 1962 and '63 state championship games. The teams met again in the 1964 state semifinals, and Wilson shifted his offense into the T-formation in the second half.

"Red knew the single wing was out of date," Carpenter says. "He'd been winning with it because no one knew how to defend it. But I'd played for coach Snavely and I knew how to defend it. We were in a six-man front against the single wing. It was a 6-2-3. Red jumped into the T on us and we didn't shift back into our 5-3. To this day I do not understand why I did not see it. We stayed in the wrong defense or they would never have beaten us.

"HI-NOC-AR" YEARBOOK PHOTO

Red was smart enough not to do it until the second half."

Carpenter was also ahead of his time in the use and emphasis of strength training. Much of the mindset through the early 1950s had been that you didn't want to become muscle-bound, but Carpenter didn't buy into that thinking.

"You couldn't play football if you didn't have upper body strength," he says. "We had a series of five exercises for them. We didn't do as much with the legs as we could have. We wanted to develop the upper body. The kids did a good job with it. They became excited about it. They saw what it could do for them."

Carpenter cites Butch Clayton, who

The 1963 cheerleaders (front row, L-R): Lindy Brice, Sarah Melvin, Betsy Neal, Pam Luper, Patricia Whaley; (second row) Gerry Dowdy, Jackie Smith, Carol Mortimer; (third row) Sharon Land, Linda Sorrell, Kathy McDiarmid, Ginger Ryals and Barbara Nelson.

as a tenth-grader "couldn't lift ten pounds. He didn't even help on the JV team. But by the time he was a senior, no one pushed him around." Clayton was the strong-side defensive tackle in the two state title wins over Reynolds.

"We annihilated the swing wing both those years, and Butch was a big reason for that," Carpenter says of Clayton, later a scholarship recruit at Carolina. "They couldn't block him."

Carpenter wrote letters to his players frequently over the summer, outlining a running and exercise regimen he wanted them to follow.

"He got you in shape and kept you in shape," says Ernest Bridges, a Blackbird on the 1959-60 teams. "Of course, a lot of stuff was different back then. They gave you two salt pills on the way out of the dressing room and you never saw any water. Now they sit under cool fans during practices and have all the water they want."

Carpenter remembers Marion Barnes being one of the leaders in the weight room.

"Marion was a tough football player," Carpenter says of Barnes, a senior in 1962 who went to prep school and then college ball at Chapel Hill. "Marion got more from that weight room than any player I had. It was a fun group. They worked like the dickens. Barnes was in there running his mouth, pushing them and got them working hard. If he'd been a couple steps faster, he'd have truly been an outstanding college football player."

Milgrom played defense for the Tar Heels as well in the mid-1960s and benefited tremendously from his high school weight room experience.

"I was ahead of the game at Chapel Hill," says Milgrom, a two-year starter for the Blackbirds at defensive end. "Marion Barnes and I brought more weights from home to Chapel Hill than they had on campus. There is no question that the high school weight training helped me against bigger kids in college."

The result of the superior scheming and conditioning was an outstanding football program.

"Maybe we did get more out of film than other coaches," Trevathan says. "Maybe our strategy was a little more creative. A lot of those old-school coaches were set in the ways they did things. They were going to do this or do that—they had for twenty years and weren't changing now.

"Our staff was young and open to new ideas. Chris brought stuff directly from Carl Snavely and Jim Tatum. Our kids could process it. If we were playing checkers, we were pretty good at it. We seemed to plan the right moves and make the right moves." ■

The Champions

Chris Carpenter's third edition of the Blackbird football team soared to an 8-0-1 record with one game left in the 1961 regular season. The Eastern 4-A Conference title was on the line when Raleigh Broughton High traveled east down U.S. Hwy 64 in early November.

The electricity crackled in Municipal Stadium as more than 6,000 fans jostled for position to watch the clash between an established power and an up-and-coming juggernaut.

It was no contest. Broughton barreled to 268 yards rushing and held Rocky Mount to minus-ten on the ground as the Caps pelted their hosts, 21-0.

"That loss really stung us," says Jep Rose, a sophomore lineman. "We were unbeaten, flying high, and they brought us down to size. They gave us a dose of reality."

Over the next twelve months, the Blackbirds grew and matured, they watched film and sweated through infinite wind sprints. They ripened as individuals and as a team. Twelve months later, they were ready to finish what they couldn't complete a year earlier.

"Broughton showed us what we could be, what a truly great high school football team looked like," says Danny Talbott, a junior on the 1961 team. "After that loss, we just strived to get better. They raised the bar."

Carpenter and Broughton coach Clyde Walker were good friends, but Carpenter was chafed somewhat at a comment from Hap Perry, the director of the North Carolina High School Athletic Association.

"Hap said Broughton was the finest high school football team he'd ever seen," Carpenter says of the Caps, who went on to win the state championship. "They were

Dennis Newell, Robert Bridgers, Marion Barnes and Butch Ferguson mount scoreboard after 1962 title game.

Managers Jim Murrill, Larry Moore and Arthur Viverette polish the Blackbirds' gold helmets.

great because they had a lot of seniors, and we were playing a lot of younger kids. The next year, I took the attitude that maybe they were the best in '61, but they weren't going to be in '62. We never lost to them again as long as I was in Rocky Mount."

Broughton had not lost a conference game in two years when Rocky Mount traveled to Raleigh on Nov. 10, 1962, for the ultimate measure in how far the Blackbird program had evolved. A crowd of 8,000 fans flocked to Riddick Stadium on the campus of N.C. State University. Rocky Mount was undersized at about twenty pounds per man across the lines, but the Blackbirds made up for the lack of girth with brains, passion and resolve.

"The football team was a bunch of guys who were not big enough, except in their hearts," says Steve Wright, a senior guard. "We had the will to win, and a lot of guys were smart enough to make it happen."

The score was tied at seven late in the game when the Blackbirds came to the line of scrimmage at the Caps' forty-three yard line. Quarterback Danny Talbott lined up in the shotgun, received the snap, cocked his arm to throw and then pulled the ball down. He raced to his left, appeared to be bottled up at the sideline by two Broughton defenders, then sliced back to the right. Bob Sides threw a block on the sideline that helped spring Talbott loose, then Talbott used his athleticism and the key blocks from assorted teammates to dart to the end zone. The Blackbirds won 13-7 and were off to the state playoffs.

"You could hold Danny down for a certain length of time," halfback Digit Laughridge says. "But odds were over the course of a game, he was going to break away. That was one of the things the coaches instilled in us. Not every play is a big play. You just have to grind and grind and look for your opening."

"The Broughton game from the year before stuck with us when it came time to play them again," Rose said. "Going into that game in '62, we wondered, 'Are we ready to beat them, or is it going to be the same as '61?' When we won, it was a big confidence boost. That really opened our minds up to the thought, 'Hey we can win this thing.'"

Indeed, they could. Rocky Mount football had officially arrived.

The team that gathered for preseason camp in August of 1962 consisted of seventeen seniors, a half dozen of whom would go on to play in college: Talbott at the University of North Carolina; halfback Wrennie Pitt, who played at Carolina before dropping football to focus on classwork; Butch Clayton, a guard who lettered in 1965 in Chapel Hill; Steve Wright, another guard who played four years at East Carolina; Marion Barnes, an end who lettered for the Tar Heels in 1966; and Bobby Jones, a

Team bus arrives in Rocky Mount after 1962 state championship win over Winston-Salem Reynolds.

tackle who played at Elon. Center Tom Parrish played on the JV basketball team at Chapel Hill. Talbott would earn All-America, All-Conference and All-State honors, while Pitt would be selected All-State and All-Conference. Senior Dennis Newell would collect first-team All-Conference accolades, as would two juniors who were lynchpins along the line, Billy Warren and John Alexander.

There were also some promising newcomers: Laughridge, Darrell Johnson, Jimmy Clack, Jerry Lundy and Steve Britt were five players who had been members of the undefeated, untied and unscored upon team from R.M. Wilson Junior High in 1961 and were elevated as tenth-graders in 1962 to the varsity.

The Blackbirds shot out of the gate with 21-0 and 33-0 wins over Henderson and Kinston to open the season, edged Goldsboro 14-12 and then dominated Wilmington 25-6 to run their record to 4-0. Next on the schedule was a trip to Fayetteville.

"Fayetteville was a military town and those guys were tough," Warren says. "A lot of those guys were raised in a military family; they were ready to go, they were disciplined. You knew when you walked on the field in Fayetteville you had a battle waiting to happen. The fans were very loud. It was a tough place to play."

The Blackbirds and Bulldogs fought to a 6-6 tie, with Fayetteville scoring a third-quarter touchdown but missing the conversion that would have put the Bulldogs ahead. The Blackbird defense stopped Fayetteville at the five yard line in the fourth quarter, when star runner Tommy Bradford was hit hard, fumbled and Tom Parrish recovered for the Blackbirds. Rocky Mount tackle Julian Fenner wondered after the game how he had acquired a sharp pain in the small of his back, then learned the next day watching film that Talbott had climbed up Fenner's back in elevating to block the crucial point-after.

"I had a rather large and painful cleat mark on my back," Fenner said. "I had made a considerable contribution to the outcome and had a scar to prove it."

Rocky Mount followed with workmanlike wins over Wilson (34-0), Durham (32-12), Tarboro (39-0) and Myers Park (27-14) to set up the conference title game at Raleigh. Their 13-7 win thrust them into a four-team state playoff. At the time there were three 4-A conferences in the state: the Eastern, Central and Western. The conferences rotated getting two representatives into the bracket, and in '62 it was the Western Conference's turn with two playoff entries—Myers Park High of Charlotte and Gastonia. Winston-Salem Reynolds was the Central Conference champion.

The draw sent the Blackbirds to Charlotte for a rematch with Myers Park, a team they'd handled two weeks earlier by a two-touchdown margin

The game drew 8,834 spectators to Memorial Stadium in Charlotte, and Carpenter's plan was to play keep-away from vaunted Mustang QB Jeff Beaver and his bevy of talented receivers like Byron Slaughter and Bud Phillips. Myers Park coach Gus Purcell was running a "basketball-on-grass" style offense long before the high-octane passing game spread throughout the 1990s.

"They had a great, great passing attack," Carpenter says. "They slaughtered everyone. I said, 'Gentlemen, we cannot afford to give them the football. Tighten it up because when we get the football, we are keeping it.'"

The Blackbirds dominated on the ground with 258 yards; Talbott threw only seven passes. Rocky Mount tucked its 21-6 victory away and returned home to prepare for the state title game against Reynolds, the 1952 and '58 state champions who were coached at the time by Shirley "Red" Wilson, who would in the 1980s become the head coach at Duke University.

Some 4,000 fans from Rocky Mount traveled to Winston Salem for the championship game at Bowman Gray Stadium. The Blackbirds dressed thirty-four players for away games and were shocked at the size of the Black Demon squad. The Reynolds squad ran through a banner hung across the goal posts at home games with a slit cut to allow one player at a time to run through. The varsity dressed out about seventy-five players, and during the playoffs it dressed out another three dozen or so from the JV team. The Reynolds band was enormous as well, with more than a hundred musicians and a sizeable accompaniment of majorettes, cheerleaders and dance-squad members.

"It looked like a hundred players," Warren says. "They kept coming and coming and coming out of the dressing room."

"I thought some of the guys in the band looked big enough to play football," Milgrom adds. "But they wore these funny looking little boots that did not cover their ankles, and I remember thinking later that if you could get a guy to wear a boot like that, he probably wouldn't have been much of a football player anyway."

The Blackbirds surprised Reynolds by coming out in a shotgun formation, and Talbott passed to Sides forty yards for a score on the Blackbirds' first possession, giving Rocky Mount a 7-0 lead less than two minutes into the game. The Blackbirds maintained complete control of the game and dominated in every statistical category: they had an 18-4 edge in first downs, 169-73 in rushing yards, 177-78 in passing and 346-151 total offense. Reynolds had no first downs in the second half and only thirty-seven yards of offense. The Blackbirds scored two TDs in the fourth quarter, Talbott running seven and

Dennis Newell (82) applies the shoulder to a Henderson running back as teammates Jimmy Clack (50), Steve Wright (64) and Digit Laughridge move in for support. The Blackbirds won the season opener, 21-0.

eleven yards for the touchdowns. The Blackbirds overcame a potentially devastating injury in the first quarter when Pitt suffered a ruptured spleen. He was taken to the hospital in Greensboro and later had his spleen removed; Pitt made a full recovery, went on to school at Chapel Hill and today is one of the top bankruptcy attorneys in Winston-Salem.

The 20-6 final score could have been even more lopsided had the Blackbirds not lost four interceptions and one fumble.

"We decided to see how they would defense the shotgun from the start," Carpenter said. "When we found we could move the ball on them, we stayed with it."

The team spent the night in Winton-Salem and left early the next morning. The bus ride was somewhat subdued as the Blackbirds worried about Pitt, and Carpenter had the driver stop in Greensboro so he could phone the hospital to check on Pitt's status.

"That was the first time playing football I ever thought about getting seriously hurt," Milgrom says. "You had cuts and bruises and sprains, but having to fix something by cutting you open got you to thinking. The way I put it out of my mind was I figured it had to have been a 'cheap shot.'"

The team arrived in Rocky Mount for a 9 a.m. celebration that included riding in the annual Christmas parade later that morning. The team bus received a police escort down Main Street to cries of "State champs!" and "We're No. 1" from hundreds of spectators.

"This is the happiest moment of my life, and I know I speak for the entire City of Rocky Mount when I say that," Mayor Billy Harrison said.

Carpenter thanked the townsfolk for their support of the team.

"Never before have I seen such support as this team received from the fans of Rocky Mount and the surrounding area," Carpenter said. "It has been just wonderful. Our dream became a reality with 150 percent effort from the team and the community."

***

The Blackbird basketball team followed much the same script as the football team during Rocky Mount's magical championship year of 1962-63—it suffered a painful loss in the playoffs the year before, learned from the defeat and ratcheted up its focus and effort for the following year.

Coach Bill Lundy's squad advanced to the finals of the state playoffs in 1962 before losing to New Hanover of Wilmington, 42-40. The Blackbirds fell behind 9-0 early in the game before steadying themselves and fighting

Brent Milgrom (88) and Marion Barnes zero in on Durham running back during win No. 7. The Blackbird defense had four shutouts and allowed one touchdown per game the last three contests.

1962 BLACKBIRD FOOTBALL

Date	Opponent	Score	H/A
Sept. 7	Henderson	21-0	A
Sept. 14	Kinston	33-0	H
Sept. 21	Goldsboro	14-12	H
Sept. 28	Wilmington	25-6	H
Oct. 5	Fayetteville	6-6	A
Oct. 12	Wilson	34-0	H
Oct. 19	Durham	32-12	A
Oct. 26	Tarboro	39-0	H
Nov. 2	Myers Park	27-14	H
Nov. 10	Raleigh Broughton	13-7	A

State Playoffs

Date	Opponent	Score	H/A
Nov. 16	Myers Park	21-6	A
Nov. 23	W-S Reynolds	20-6	A

1962 State 4-A Champions

Front Row (L-R): Danny Talbott, Wrennie Pitt, Craig Quick, Steve Kelly, Russell Hall, Steve Britt, Dennis Newell, Marion Barnes.

Second Row: Chris Carpenter, Darrell Johnson, Robert Bridgers, Jimmy Arrington, Wayne Daughtridge, Bill Bonner, Buddy Elmore, Mike Branch, Henry Trevathan.

Third Row: Allen Wester, Julian Fenner, Butch Ferguson, Digit Laughridge, Bob Sides, Billy Warren, Steve Wright, Tom Parrish, Wesley Ballou.

Fourth Row: Joe Phillips, Skip Thompson, John Alexander, David Parker, Brent Milgrom, Bobby Jones, Jep Rose, Butch Clayton, Marvin Pike, Wayne Bulluck, Tommy Cheshire.

CHARLES S. KILLEBREW COLLECTION, BRASWELL MEMORIAL LIBRARY

Billy Warren battles for loose ball as Tom Parrish (24) and Jimmy Clack (50) hover nearby vs. Durham High.

back, only to fall two points short.

"We were so close that year," guard Danny Talbott says. "It was like football—we had a major disappointment one year and the next year won a championship."

With four of five starters still involved in football playoffs through Thanksgiving weekend, Lundy's goal for the 1962-63 season was to develop the team slowly and carefully, forsaking any goals of regular-season success and instead looking to peak at playoff time.

"Last year, I think we had pushed a little too hard during the regular season," Lundy said. "We are a comparatively small school against some of the schools we face, and I think we wore ourselves out. We were physically whipped by tournament time. We just didn't have the manpower."

"We played our first basketball game on a Tuesday after our last football game on a Friday," says Tom Parrish, a lineman in football and forward in basketball. "We were such a small school that guys had to play two or three sports for us to field a team. We put on our basketball uniforms, but we were still 'playing football' until about Christmas time. It took a while to shed the football mindset and learn to play basketball all over again."

Lundy was in his seventeenth year as Rocky Mount basketball coach and by now had certainly established his system and his bedrock of core fundamentals.

His teams were predicated on working the ball inside on offense, and they were experts at probing zone defenses. They played tight man-to-man defense, and it was a capital offense to allow an opponent to drive the baseline. The Blackbirds worked endlessly on switching and communication techniques on defense.

"Another big thing was rebounding and boxing out," says forward Bill Warren. "We had to be good at boxing out because we didn't have the size."

Lundy was a disciple of long-time Oklahoma A&M coach Henry Iba and West Virginia coach Fred Schaus. He learned from Ray Mears, the young coach at the University of Tennessee, how to figure offensive efficiency based on points scored, number of possessions and time of possession.

"Dad wanted you to milk the clock and then get a good shot," says Mike Lundy, one of two sons active on Blackbird teams in the 1950s and '60s. "Every summer he'd go to clinics and come back with something new. He was always learning new stuff, but the basics to him were the same. Work the ball, block out and play good defense."

Lundy wouldn't stand for anything resembling hot-dogging, whether intentional or not. Talbott one day in practice his junior year was blocked on a drive along the baseline, and the only way to get rid of the ball was to flip it around his back. His teammate was not expecting the pass, and the ball hit him in the nose and bounced out-of-bounds.

"Don't do that again," Lundy said in a stern voice.

It wasn't long after that Talbott found himself caught in a similar jam—a defender was in his face, had the angles covered and left Talbott with no choice but to whisk it around his back to a teammate, who caught the ball and laid it in for two points.

"Talbott, that's twenty-five laps after practice," Lundy said.

Talbott fumed as he ran round and round the court.

The next year, Talbott was gone and Jimmy Arrington was the point guard, and he drew Lundy's ire by throwing a pass behind his back in the third game of the season. For the rest of the year, as the team was about to leave the locker room before each game, Lundy would turn to assistant coach Dudley Whitley.

"Coach, take ole Jimbo back there and let him get all those behind-the-back passes out of his system," Lundy said, then watched as Arrington threw twenty-five passes around his backside to Whitley.

"Coach Lundy was a no-nonsense kind of guy," Talbott says. "But he was also a great teacher. And he was patient. He'd stay out there all night with you if you needed him."

Talbott was challenged at the beginning of each basketball season to convert his right-hand passing motion with a football into a smooth shooting motion for basketball. It wasn't always a smooth transition.

"The football comes off your index finger when you throw a spiral, and then I'd have a tendency to shoot the basketball like that," Talbott says. "It was ugly at times early in the season. Coach Lundy was great helping me with drills to get my shooting motion down."

Lundy tried to make practice fun, using colored Tootsie Pops as prizes for making a certain percentage of free throws. He also created game situations, putting a player on the foul line and outlining a set of crucial game circumstances.

"Then you'd be into your motion and he'd drop a quarter on the floor or shuffle his feet behind you to distract you," Whitley says.

Lundy developed a system for attacking zone defenses and even drew the attention of North Carolina coach Frank McGuire, who visited Rocky Mount to learn from Lundy.

"That's a pretty good compliment, Frank McGuire coming to a high school coach to learn something about attacking a zone," Warren says.

"Lundy's system of attacking a zone was one of best things I'd ever seen," Whitley said. "We would wear a zone out. Danny was out front at the point with the bas-

Tom Parrish (24) was one of the better shooters on the 1962-63 state championship team.

CHARLES S. KILLEBREW COLLECTION, BRASWELL MEMORIAL LIBRARY

Harold Earnhardt reaches for ball while Robert Ricks (12) and Tom Parrish move in vs. Fayetteville.

ketball. He'd draw people to him and get the ball where it needed to be."

As soon as football was over, Lundy had his team. Included on the roster were seniors Talbott, Jimmy Coats, Robert Ricks, Tom Parrish, Jim McChesney and Allen Wester; juniors Warren, George Watson and Jep Rose; and sophomore Henry Strickland. Jimmy Clack was a sophomore who originally played on the JV team but was moved up during the season to the varsity. Warren started with the varsity, was sent to the JV team early in the year to get some playing experience, then was elevated back to the varsity in February in time for an important game against Durham.

Clack was the tallest at 6-3. Parrish was 6-2 and Warren 6-1 along the front line. Talbott and Parrish were the most experienced players, as both played varsity ball as sophomores and were starting by mid-season of the 1960-61 season.

"No one on the team could dunk it," Talbott says. "We weren't impressive physically. But we were a disciplined team. You played defense. You played man-to-man from the get-go. You played in his face. You passed the ball and you looked for the lay-up. You knew how to box out on rebounds. We were not fancy, but we were efficient."

Warren recalls playing Asheville in the 1962 state tournament and battling a distinct size disadvantage.

"They had guys 6-6 and 6-7," he says. "I saw them walk out on the court and said, 'Good God, we're going to have our hands full.' And we did, but we out-rebounded them. We were just quicker, we boxed out and we played tough, hard defense. Those things always pulled us through."

The Blackbirds were 4-6 in league play and tied for fourth place as the regular season wound down. They were fighting with Wilson and Raleigh for fourth in the league tournament; finishing fourth instead of fifth would land them a home-court game in the tournament. Their starting lineup had evolved to Talbott and Ricks at guard, Warren and Parrish at forward and Clack at center. Ricks was the defensive stopper, Clack and Warren tough defenders and rebounders, and Talbott and Parrish were the playmakers with the ball.

"Clack came on real strong at the end," Rose says. "At that age you can develop a lot in two to three months. Clack was a fabulous athlete. He was coordinated and so strong. He was naturally strong before we did much with weights."

And Talbott, of course, was the clutch performer. In a Feb. 12 home game against Broughton, Talbott stole the ball and raced up court for the game-winning layup with sixteen seconds to play in a 47-46 victory.

"A little more court discipline, a little better scoring

Sophomore center Jimmy Clack launches baseline jumper against Wilmington during two-point loss.

balance and a little better team defense," Lundy said. "We're not far away in these things, and just a little improvement could make a big difference."

The Blackbirds beat Durham 62-51 and then pounded Wilson 68-49 in the final two games and finished 6-6 in the league.

"It's the second straight real fine game for us," Lundy said. "And this has to rank as our best game of the year. This year we had a lot of tough breaks. I think we lost four games by a total of four points. We felt we'd be all right as long as we could finish fourth. The tournament was what counted with us."

The Eastern 4-A Conference tournament was held in Wilmington, and the Blackbirds hammered Wilson again, this time by sixteen points, in the first round. Next up was New Hanover on the Wildcats' home court. Talbott hit a jumper from the corner with four seconds left and Rocky Mount escaped with a 45-44 win—its first in seventeen years at New Hanover. "That win definitely gave us the inspiration," Talbott said.

Rocky Mount lost to Durham 50-46 in the tournament final and entered the eight-team state 4-A tournament at Greensboro Senior High as the second seed from the Eastern Conference. The Blackbirds faced Gastonia in the first round, and Talbott scored twenty points in leading his team to an uneventful 49-30 win.

The Blackbirds' semifinal opponent was Burlington High, a team with an impressive 17-3 record and a leader in the form of future N.C. State football star and University of Georgia head coach Jim Donnan. Warren and Clack delivered eighteen-point performances and Talbott chipped in sixteen as Rocky Mount rolled to a 72-58 victory. Ricks was the defensive stopper on Donnan, who scored only nine points and was 4-for-16 from the field.

"What a determined bunch of battlers those kids were tonight," Lundy said. "Desire—they've got mountains of it. Burlington made it mighty tough under the boards, but we took it and gave a little more back."

The championship game was played Saturday and pitted Rocky Mount against Greensboro Grimsley, who was coached by Bob Jamieson, one of the legendary coaches in North Carolina prep circles.

"They still don't believe in us up here, but tonight we hope to convince them once and for all that we're for real," Lundy said.

Jamieson was not among those needing convincing. After all, the Whirlies had lost to Rocky Mount 56-35 in the state tournament the previous year.

"Anybody who sells this Rocky Mount team short is making a mistake," Jamieson said.

Parrish scored eighteen first half points in staking Rocky Mount to a 27-16 lead at intermission. Grimsley's

Billy Warren battles for ball under hoop during 11-point win over Durham as Birds geared up for playoffs.

Pat Moriarty led a third-quarter rally with six straight field goals as the Whirlies outscored the Blackbirds 19-6 to take a 35-33 lead.

"The boys simply refused to panic under pressure," Lundy said. "They could have quit when they lost that eleven-point lead. And they could have quit when Talbott fouled out."

Talbott left the game with 1:10 to play. Parrish scored with fifty-three seconds in regulation to force a tie at 46-46. Then he opened the overtime with a bucket and Ricks sank two foul shots to give the Blackbirds a 50-46 edge. But Grimsley tied it as John Hedrick was fouled on successive trips down the floor and made four free throws.

The Blackbirds froze the ball with forty-eight seconds to play, and Lundy called for a play off a double-post set, with Parrish getting the ball near the key. He could shoot, drive, or pass the ball. He took the pass and was quickly double-teamed, but he couldn't find anyone open with a good shot. So Parrish elevated for the jumper and got it off. The ball hit the front of the rim, then took its time bouncing to the back of the rim. That extra bounce threw off the timing of the Grimsley defenders, and Clack got position, snared the rebound and stuck it back as the buzzer sounded, giving Rocky Mount a 52-50 win.

"That team caught fire under Bill Lundy," says Bob Williams, the sports editor of the *Rocky Mount Telegram*.

"They had a drill, drill, drill mentality. Danny had great command of all aspects of the game. Parrish was a terrific shooter. Clack was a big, rugged guy. He had not developed, but he came alive in the state tournament. Nobody would have ever thought that team would be a champion, but it all came together at the right time."

Warren and Parrish both credit Lundy's fundamentals with helping Clack get into sound rebounding posture for the game-winning score.

"That was all Lundy's fundamentals—box out, box out, box out," Warren says. "We especially worked hard on the offensive boards. I got something like seventeen points in one of the state tournament games, and most of it was rebounding inside and putting it back up."

"Coach taught us that if get our butt on our man, we *will* get the rebound," Parrish says. "They can't come over the top of you, and if they do, they'll pick up a foul."

Linwood Clack made the 260-mile round trip to Greensboro in one day to watch his son Jimmy play, despite the knowledge from his doctor that he had developed heart disease and was susceptible to heart attacks. When young Clack arrived home the day after the championship game, he found his father on the front porch, cutting up fifty copies of the *Telegram* with the bold headline, "Jim Clack Wins State Championship" and sending all of them to friends and relatives.

1962-63 State 4-A Champions

Front Row (L-R): Jimmy Coats, Jimmy Clack, Tom Parrish, Danny Talbott, Billy Warren and Robert Ricks. **Second Row**: Chuck Taylor, Chuck Robbins, Ronald Barnes, Frank Harrison, Jim McChesney, Harold Earnhardt, Allen Wester and Jep Rose.

1962-3 BLACKBIRD BASKETBALL

Dec. 7	Kinston	49-55	H	Jan. 23	Goldsboro	70-54	H
Dec. 14	Patrick Henry	47-33	A	Jan. 25	Durham	51-64	A
Dec. 15	William Fleming	55-36	A	Jan. 29	Wilson	54-56	H
Dec. 18	Kinston	44-37	A	Feb. 1	Fayetteville	47-49	A
Dec. 19	Greenville	44-37	A	Feb. 5	Danville	52-46	A
Jan. 4	Greenville	66-24	H	Feb. 9	Wilmington	48-50	H
Jan. 8	Fayetteville	52-47	H	Feb. 12	Raleigh Broughton	47-46	H
Jan. 11	Wilmington	35-36	A	Feb. 15	Goldsboro	45-48	A
Jan. 15	Danville	48-41	H	Feb. 19	Durham	62-51	H
Jan. 18	Raleigh Broughton	44-40	A	Feb. 22	Wilson	68-49	A

Eastern 4-A Conference Tournament

Feb. 28	Wilson	63-47	H
March 1	Wilmington	45-44	A
March 2	Durham	46-50	A (Wilmington)

State Tournament

March 7	Gastonia	49-30	Greensboro
March 8	Burlington	72-58	Greensboro
March 9	Greensboro Grimsley	52-50	Greensboro

"I want you to know how proud I am of you, even if I'm not here to tell you," Linwood told Jimmy.

Linwood died less than a week later of a heart attack.

"To this very day, I still picture him surrounded with those articles that he so lovingly and pridefully clipped and sent," Clack said more than three decades later.

Dean Smith, only one year into what would be a legendary tenure as the head coach at the University of North Carolina, spoke at the Sportsman's Club banquet in April honoring team.

"One of the finest things about this team is that it came back from early losses to win the state championship," Smith said. "This was a team that believed in winning. You have a winning tradition here at Rocky Mount Senior High.

"These boys are better off for having competed," Smith added. "Everybody wants to win, but just playing the game has its value. Competing gives a boy a goal to reach for, a goal that carries both immediate and long range values."

***

Two down, one to go?

Rocky Mount had won titles in football and basketball, so spring arrived and now the focus was on coach Dudley Whitley and the baseball team.

"We had no thoughts of winning a third one when the season started," Whitley says. "We had three sophomores start in baseball. We had modest hopes going into the baseball season. But after football and basketball won, it put a little more pressure on us."

Whitley was in his fourth season as the Blackbirds' baseball coach. His team would be built around—what else?—the all-around athleticism of Danny Talbott, who pitched and played third base and hit for a hefty percentage. Jimmy Daniels was an experienced and cool-headed catcher and a plus-.300 hitter who would go on to play baseball at East Carolina; he was also a long-time battery mate of Talbott's, dating back to Small Fry baseball a decade earlier.

"Danny could throw a baseball harder than any human I'd ever seen—except for maybe Catfish Hunter," Daniels says. "I can still remember my hand swelling and how much it hurt after catching Danny. I've caught a lot of guys, from high school and American Legion ball to playing at ECU, and I never caught anyone who could throw harder."

There were plenty of good players around Talbott, just as there had been for football and basketball. The infield featured Dennis Newell at first base, Eddie Allen at shortstop and Digit Laughridge at third. The outfield included Darrell Johnson in center and Billy Warren in left. When Talbott wasn't pitching, he played third, and Laughridge either pitched or moved to right field. Craig Quick and Jimmy Coats both played second base, though Coats moved into the lineup on a regular basis as the playoffs evolved. Skip Thompson and Allen Ricks were used in right field.

"We had only five seniors on the team, and four of them were starters," Whitley said. "We were fortunate in that three sophomores played really good ball for us. We started out with only one experienced pitcher, but then two sophomores came through and did a good job."

Whitley had the most "rah-rah" qualities of any of Rocky Mount's head coaches, but he was cut from the same cloth as Chris Carpenter and Bill Lundy in building a program predicated on fundamentals and painstaking attention to detail.

"Dudley always said that games were won and lost on routine plays," Laughridge says. "Do the routine plays and the spectacular plays will take care of themselves. That's pretty good advice. I took that to college and beyond: Take care of the routine plays.

"He also managed his players well. He knew who and where and when to put the guys. He knew all of us inside and out. He knew the round pegs for the round holes and the square pegs for the square holes."

Whitley's exuberance was manifested in his hustling.

"Dudley was a hustler and he wanted you to hustle," Bill Warren says. "Dudley was always hustling for the extra base, running everything out. He was a stickler for hitting the cut-off man, doing the little things right that added up over the season.

"You knew Dudley was going to make the right calls. He wasn't going to make a lot of mistakes to get you beat. His teams were going to be fundamentally sound."

The Blackbirds were 7-2 through early May and Whitley noted those elements of Baseball 101 in a midseason comment to the *Telegram*: "Our improvement appears to be in things like smarter base running and throwing to the right base. We've improved in the things that win ball games."

Their next outing was in Wilson, and the Blackbirds were in control of the game from the outset, coasting to a 21-3 win. But the victory was costly as Talbott suffered a hairline fracture in his left hand when hit by a pitch in the third inning.

"The pitch didn't look like it was coming that hard," Talbott said. "But then suddenly it just seemed to take off and come at me."

Talbott was benched for a week in recovery but returned to the lineup as the Blackbirds closed out the regular season with an 11-5 overall record and 9-4 mark

Little League teams like this one set the stage for future Blackbird success. Front row (L-R): Bill Robbins, unidentified, Tommy Creech, Frankie Langley, Jimmy Coats, Chuck Taylor and Chuck Robbins. Back row: Mike Taylor, Graham Campbell, Bill Bonner, David Parker, Brent Milgrom, Bobby McMillan, Darrell Johnson and coach Bobby Gorham.

in the Eastern 4-A Conference, tied for first with Goldsboro. That necessitated a one-game playoff for the league title and berth in the state playoffs. Sophomore Jimmy Arrington pitched a three-hitter and the Blackbirds rallied with four runs in the seventh inning to beat Goldsboro, 5-3.

"You can never give up on these boys," Whitley said. "They're made of good stuff and they just won't quit."

The momentum was building on the team and within the community to continue the string of championships.

"We had a lot of motivation," Daniels says today. "Everyone was saying, 'Gotta keep it going, gotta keep it going.' That's all we could hear, day in and day out.

"I'll be honest, we had a good baseball team, but we weren't necessarily better than a lot of teams we played. The football team was by far the best team, no question. The basketball team was good, but maybe not the best. They got hot and played great at the right time. We were more like the basketball team."

The Blackbirds traveled to Charlotte to play East Mecklenburg in the semifinals of the state playoffs; they were armed with the superior batting averages of Talbott at .444, Daniels at .419, Newell at .405, Warren at .350 and Darrell Johnson at .310. Talbott was the leading pitcher with a 6-2 record and 1.35 ERA. Arrington threw an excellent curve ball and was 3-0 with a 1.46 ERA.

Talbott pitched the opener for the Blackbirds and was in control for six innings, allowing just five hits and one run. He began wearing a golf glove on his left hand after the break earlier in the year, and the glove had become moist with sweat when he came to the plate in the top of the seventh inning (the last in a standard high school game of seven innings). Talbott tried to hold up his swing on one pitch and the bat slipped in his hand, popping open the bone crack that had not completely healed. He was taken to the hospital, his season presumably over. Arrington pitched the final inning and picked up a save as Rocky Mount collected a 5-4 win.

Game two was played immediately afterward, and Arrington went the distance for the Blackbirds in a losing cause, also by a 5-4 margin.

Whitley assigned Laughridge to the mound the next day in game three. Laughridge blanked East Mecklenburg for five innings, then gave up three hits and three runs as the Eagles cut a 4-0 deficit to 4-3. Watching in the dugout, Talbott told Whitley he thought he could pitch. Assistant coach Johnny Stott had an oversized glove that Talbott was able to put on his left hand, over the cast.

"Are you sure?" Whitley pressed.

"Yes, sir, I know I can," Talbott answered.

"Okay, give it a try and see what you can do."

Talbott felt comfortable in the bullpen, so Whitley inserted him in relief with one out in the sixth inning wearing a long-sleeve shirt to cover the cast on his left hand that stretched nearly to his elbow. East Mecklenburg coach Dave Jones protested, saying the cast "was a distraction," but the umpires allowed Talbott to continue to pitch. He gave up a single and then struck out the next batter and got a grounder to force the runner at second and end the inning. In the seventh, Talbott gave up a single and then struck out three Eagles in a row to get the save and send the Blackbirds into the state championship series.

"It was some of my best stuff ever," Talbott said.

"Even one-armed, Danny Talbott is still too much for most of his opponents," *The Charlotte Observer* said in its report of the game.

The team was now on a roll and was building on its success in football and basketball as it traveled to Greensboro to face Page High in a best-of-three series.

"We had some guys off the state championship football team, the championship basketball team, who knew what it was like to win, what it took to win," Laughridge says. "When we got in a crunch, they took the reins mentally and helped the rest of the team pull through."

"After we won in Charlotte, we just had that feel, that momentum," Daniels adds. "We looked at what football and basketball had done and said, 'We've got a real opportunity.'"

Arrington pitched a five-hitter in leading the Blackbirds to a victory in the first game, 2-1, with a triple by Allen Ricks and a double by Coats driving in the runs. With Talbott not available, Whitley was forced to look toward another sophomore for the second game, either Laughridge or Steve Peterson. He opted to go with Peterson in order to have Laughridge available for game three if needed. Peterson had pitched only one and two-thirds innings all year and had struggled with control problems. But he pitched well in the clutch of the title game, walking only two Page batters over seven innings and retiring Page in order over the final two innings.

"I said if he didn't walk more than five, Steve would do all right," Whitley said after the game. "That's what he did. Steve was a picture of concentration. He really battled. He was hit hard at times, but he never threw as hard as he could because we told him to throw strikes."

"Steve put a lot of junk on the ball," Daniels says today. "He had a great curve ball. He was hard to hit. He couldn't throw it hard enough to break a window, but he put it all together in the last game."

Daniels had a two-run homer, Allen made timely plays at shortstop, Ricks was six-for-14 over the two playoff series and Coats emerged with a three-for-seven bat-

Smiles all around after 5-3 win over Goldsboro for conference title (clockwise from lower-right): Danny Talbott, Jimmy Arrington, Jimmy Daniels, Dudley Whitley, Johnny Stott and Jimmy Armstrong.

Catcher Jimmy Daniels leads the Blackbirds off the diamond following state championship win.

1963 BLACKBIRD BASEBALL

March 22	C.B. Aycock	5-2	A	April 26	Raleigh Enloe	5-4	H
March 29	S. Edgecombe	7-0	H	May 2	Wilson	21-3	A
April 2	Raleigh Enloe	2-6	A	May 3	Wilson	5-6	H
April 5	Durham	11-2	H	May 7	Fayetteville	8-5	A
April 11	Fayetteville	5-0	H	May 10	Wilmington	2-3	H
April 16	Wilmington	9-2	A	May 14	Broughton	9-6	H
April 19	Broughton	5-10	A	May 27	Goldsboro	2-3	A
April 23	Goldsboro	5-3	H	May 22	Durham	7-0	A

Eastern Conference Playoff
May 25   Goldsboro   5-3   Wilson

State Semifinal Series
June 3   East Mecklenburg   5-4   Charlotte
June 3   East Mecklenburg   4-5   Charlotte
June 4   East Mecklenburg   4-3   Charlotte

State Championship Series
June 7   Greensboro Page   2-1   Greensboro
June 8   Greensboro Page   11-6   Greensboro

1963 State 4-A Champions

Front Row (L-R): Manager Bernie Capps, Digit Laughridge, Craig Quick, Jimmy Coats, Eddie Allen, Allen Ricks and Joe Thomas.

Second Row: Skip Thompson, Dennis Newell, Jimmy Arrington, Danny Talbott, Jimmy Daniels, Johnny Brooks and Joe Swaim.

Third Row: Coach Dudley Whitley, manager Tommy Jenkins, Darrell Johnson, Steve Peterson, Billy Warren, Bill Blaylock, Ray Todd, managers Kenneth Rackley and Wilbur Bryant.

CHARLES S. KILLEBREW COLLECTION, BRASWELL MEMORIAL LIBRARY

ting performance in the championship series. The Blackbirds exploded for six runs in the sixth inning of the second game against Page, and the result was an 11-6 win for the state title.

The team returned home and another celebration ensued. The town was getting good at this.

"These fellows were great," Whitley said. "They'll never let you down. I just held on this season and went for a ride."

"The guys were good, clean, wholesome boys," says Daniels, whose uncle Charlie was the long-time director of the YMCA leagues that spawned many of the Blackbird players. "They were good ball players and loved the game. A couple were really talented, the rest were really good.

"Looking back, you'd have to say it was just destiny. The first two teams did it, why not a third?

***

The Danny Talbott era had come to an end.

Three years of Talbott getting the clutch yards, baskets and base hits had built to a glorious crescendo as Talbott took his considerable skills ninety miles to the west and the University of North Carolina.

It was time to move on.

"All of the seniors knew that we had set a new level," Bill Warren says of the mindset approaching the 1963 football season. "We had raised the bar and we wanted to win all three state championships again. Replacing Danny would be tough, but we took it as a challenge. It wasn't pressure from anybody else. It was just us wanting to continue to have an outstanding football team."

"We thought we'd be good, but quarterback was really uncertain," adds David Parker, a guard on offense and tackle on defense. "Talbott was such an outstanding leader, someone you relied upon to always make the right decisions. He was so error-free. We didn't know what the offense would be like without him."

The roster had forty-two players, with nineteen seniors, twelve lettermen and six starters returning. Tackle John Alexander was the captain. The backfield returned two starters—halfbacks Digit Laughridge and fullback Wayne Daughtridge. Junior Steve Britt was the new quarterback following Talbott's departure. Defensive backs Laughridge and Darrell Johnson, another offensive starter at halfback, were the only players going both ways to open the year. The talent was there, for sure. Two future UNC players dotted the lineup—defensive end Brent Milgrom and two-way end Warren. Laughridge, Jimmy Clack and junior linebacker/QB Jimmy Arrington would play at Wake Forest, and

David Parker blocks for Craig Quick as Blackbirds look to establish some offensive consistency during 1963 season.

PHOTO COURTESY NORMA PARKER

Johnson would earn a scholarship to South Carolina.

The opening win over Henderson by a 20-0 score set a tempo that would persist for much of the year. On defense, there were no problems as the Blackbirds would essentially suffocate every opponent. On offense, the challenge of finding a new quarterback would take some time to solve.

Britt started the opener at quarterback but Joe Swaim and Arrington played as well; between them, there were ten fumbles on center and ball-carrier exchanges, and four of them were recovered by Henderson. Swaim was the quarterback on the two Blackbird offensive scoring drives. But Henderson's offense was inept against a stout Blackbird defense; Henderson had only four first downs and seventy-nine yards of offense, and Clack intercepted a pass and returned it ninety-five yards for a touchdown.

The Homecoming Court presented at the 1963 Raleigh Broughton game included (L-R): Ginger Ryals, Jackie Smith and Barbara Nelson.

"Defensively, we did a terrific job, but offensively we have a lot of work to do," Carpenter said. "Our ball-handling was terrible and we didn't block well. The center has to change his snap for each quarterback. We're going to have to settle on one quarterback and stick with him."

The Blackbirds' thirteen-game winning streak ended on Friday the thirteenth—in a drizzling rain in Kinston on the second Friday of the season. A five-yard Blackbird punt in the second quarter gave the Red Devils excellent field position, and they quickly converted with a thirty-three yard scoring pass in the second quarter from Billy Taylor to halfback Bob Koehler. The Blackbirds got as deep as the Kinston thirty yard line three times in the game, but they lost the ball on an interception and two foiled fourth-down gambles. Kinston emerged with a 7-0 win.

"Kinston was a wake-up call," Laughridge says. "That game told us we were absolutely mortal, that we'd better take things more seriously. We'd been resting on our laurels. Kinston was just good enough to beat us. We knew we were going to have to play better than the year before."

"There was a lot of uncertainty on offense after the Kinston game," Parker adds. "We didn't move the ball at all. We kept making errors and mistakes. The offense wasn't jelling. The quarterback play was very erratic."

Carpenter remembers the coaching staff taking a hard line after that game.

"We kicked some butt after Kinston," he says today. "We had no business losing to them. We came back and our kids wished to hell they'd never lost to Kinston. We head-knocked and banged all week. Jimmy Clack came out of practice on Monday holding his shoulder and I said, 'What have I done now?' I was afraid I'd ruined the whole season."

Fortunately, Clack's injury wasn't serious and he returned to the practice field on Thursday. The Blackbirds were scheduled to travel to Goldsboro to meet a team they had edged by two points the previous year. "This is a crucial game for us," Carpenter said before the game. "We feel it's a game we *have* to win."

"We knew Goldsboro was good," Parker says today. "They had been tough the year before. They were a single-wing team and those teams were hard to play with all the misdirection stuff. There was a fair amount of doubt as I remember when we went down to Goldsboro."

The Blackbirds were warming up when they heard the Goldsboro High students singing the song *Danny Boy* in mock tribute to the defending state champions who were struggling without their departed hero. But the Blackbirds shut Goldsboro down and emerged with a 13-0 victory.

The Blackbirds built on that win by hammering Wilmington 26-6 the following week in Municipal Stadium. Laughridge sped fifty-five yards for one score, and Swaim hit Warren on TD passes of fifteen and nine yards and ran one in himself. The defense was stout as usual, holding Wilmington to fifty-one yards rushing until the final eight minutes, when the substitutes entered the game.

Next up: Fayetteville, the No. 1 team in the state.

"We have continued to make mistakes and have managed to get by most of the time despite them," Carpenter told the weekly meeting of the Sportsman's Club. "Against Fayetteville, however, it will be a different story. Every mistake we make against this team is going to cost us."

Municipal Stadium was bursting with more than 6,000 fans to see a 20-13 Rocky Mount triumph. Two big

Backfield mates through three seasons were Digit Laughridge (L) and Darrell Johnson; the former collects a post-season trophy and the latter some attention from Barbara Nelson.

defensive plays early in the game staked the Blackbirds to a 14-0 lead as Arrington recovered a fumble at the twenty and then intercepted a pass and returned it sixty-four yards to the one. Assistant coach Don Stallings worked tackle Lee Pearce into a froth during the week, chiding Pearce that Fayetteville fullback Tommy Bradford was going to flatten Pearce all night.

"The coaches knew how to get under your skin, to psyche you up," says Pearce. "I had one of my best games ever that night. I don't know what the stats were, but I hit Bradford over and over again. I was 175 pounds and he was 225 and I got the best of him that night."

Pearce was named "Blackbird of the Week" for his efforts, a much-coveted honor as the Rosenbloom-Levy men's store gave the winner a Gantt shirt.

"I think we hit Fayetteville a little harder than they expected," Carpenter said. "We rammed the ball right down their throats the first time we got it."

One of the subplots of the game was Warren and Alexander teaming on the right side of the offensive front to dominate one of the Bulldogs' outstanding defensive linemen. Later that winter, Rocky Mount was preparing to play basketball at Fayetteville when a stout young man came nosing around the Blackbird dressing room.

"You got a guy named Warren here?" he asked.

Warren responded, "Yeah, I'm him."

"Well, I wanna talk to you."

Warren was wondering what was coming. He girded up and said, "Okay, I'm here."

The fellow introduced himself as Ronnie Peele, extended his hand and said, "I just want to shake your hand because you two blocked me like no one else did all year. You had me confused and kept switching the way you were blocking. You guys beat my brains out and I just wanted to come say hello."

Warren and Peele became friends, and Peele even signed Warren's *Hi-Noc-Ar* yearbook over a photo from that game that showed Warren blocking Peele.

Halfway through the season, the Blackbirds were 4-1 and the defense would ratchet up its efforts for the homestretch. Beginning with a 42-0 out of Wilson in week six, the defense played five games allowing only two TDs.

Meanwhile, Arrington took control at quarterback.

"The team developed confidence in Jimmy," Parker says. "He was a good ball-handler, a good faker, made good decisions and turned out to be a better runner than the other guys.

"We had a great defense that year. But without Danny, it took a while for the offense to jell. No one had the physical skills of Danny. We played three quarterbacks and none of them mastered the system at first. Eventually Jimmy took over and made things happen."

As Arrington established himself, more options opened for halfbacks Laughridge and Johnson.

"When Darrell and I were playing halfback, it left Jim a lot of room to run because they couldn't cover all three of us," Laughridge says. "Jim was an excellent passer. To me he was a thinker on the field. He was a smart runner. No matter the situation, Jim never panicked. There was a sense among all of us in the backfield that if one play didn't work, we had another that would work."

Another key to the season was Laughridge's success on punt returns—many of those yards behind Warren's precise blocking.

"Billy rang more bells than St. Mary's," Laughridge says. "He was the first guy to set up the wall on the return. It was almost like a science. Every return, you could count on Billy cleaning someone's clock. As a player, you rarely heard the crowd, but I remember one game when Billy knocked a guy into the nickel seats and the crowd exploded. I wondered as the season went along how the opposing coaches could convince anyone to take the outside coverage. They knew what was coming."

Rocky Mount beat Durham by a touchdown and handled Greenville easily before traveling to Charlotte for what had become an annual meeting with Myers Park. The game was played in a hard rain on a muddy field, and the only score of the game came on Mustang fullback Herb Goins' eighty-yard run. At least three Blackbirds had good shots on Goins, two of them the interior linemen, Lee Pearce and Monk Reams.

"I hit Goins at the line and he slipped off me like an eel," says Pearce. "I was face down in the mud, looked up and Monk was right there beside me. I said, 'Monk, why didn't you get him?' Monk said, 'Why didn't *you* get him?' By that time Goins was crossing the goal line."

The Blackbirds were 7-2 entering in the final game of the regular season, a home contest with conference rival Raleigh Broughton, but were still unbeaten in the league as the losses to Kinston and Myers Park were outside of the Eastern 4-A.

Broughton had only one offensive threat all night, that coming when the Caps took the opening kickoff of the second half and drove inside the Blackbird ten yard line. They went for the score on fourth-and-two at the seven. Parker and Craig Quick, the tackle and cornerback, respectively, on the right side, suspected Raleigh would come with the off-tackle play to their side. Parker slanted in the direction of the play, Quick shot the line and they met the ball-carrier four yards deep in the backfield to stop the threat and secure the 6-0 win— Rocky Mount's first perfect conference record.

Rocky Mount intercepted three passes and capitalized on two bad center snaps on punts to hammer

Brent Milgrom, David Parker, Craig Quick, John Alexander, Billy Warren say Birds No. 1 after 1963 victory.

Greensboro Page 42-0 at home in the first round of the state playoffs, then set sights on Winston-Salem Reynolds for the second straight year.

"I really didn't think it could be that easy," Carpenter said. "Page has some good ball players, but they made it really easy for us."

The Blackbird Special train ran to Winston-Salem on Friday, Nov. 22, 1963, and the team boarded its Trailways bus for the trip west. At 11:30 a.m. Eastern Time, a thousand miles away in Dallas, President John F. Kennedy was shot and pronounced dead half an hour later. The Blackbirds had just checked into their motel in Winston-Salem, and Carpenter was headed to his room when he heard two maids scream out from the room they were cleaning. They had the television on and had just gotten news of the assassination. Carpenter went around to each player as they were having their ankles taped and told them about the shooting.

"Something tragic has happened," Carpenter said. "The President has been shot and killed. It's a tragedy, but we have work to do. So let's stay focused, let's get it done and then we'll mourn."

"Coach kept us focused even though he knew some of the guys would be upset," Warren says.

The Blackbirds and Black Demons kicked off in front of a crowd of some 12,000 fans, half of them having made the trip from Rocky Mount. As always, the Blackbirds took the field confident and armed with a game plan they believed would result in victory if they executed their plays properly.

Exhibit A: The plan to stop a deadly wingback reverse that Reynolds had used throughout the year.

One of the base plays in the single wing offense was to have the tailback take the direct snap from the center and run the ball to the right, behind the power blocking to the strong side of the formation. Reynolds developed that play and then, off of it, would have the tailback hand off to the wingback coming back around to the left.

"They were killing people with that play," says Parker, who at right tackle was dead in the sights of the play's direction. "They were getting huge chunks of yards. Coach Carpenter and coach Stallings told me, if nothing else, take a knee and knock the first guy down. They said if I felt like I could stop him, if I could stand him up with a forearm, then do that and then spin into the hole. Reynolds tried that play four times, and every time I stood the guy up, spun into the hole and there was the ball-carrier. I think they lost six yards on those plays.

"That was all coaching. They saw it on film and knew how to teach us to stop it."

Exhibit B: The introduction of a halfback pass into the offensive arsenal to take advantage of Reynolds' aggressive pursuit.

The Blackbirds' second score was set up when Laughridge took a lateral pass from Arrington in the flat, then lofted a pass downfield to Jeff Croom for thirty-five yards to the Reynolds twenty-nine. That play set up Arrington-to-Laughridge on the next snap for what proved to be the winning score. Jerry Lundy's point after gave the Blackbirds a 14-7 lead. Late in the game, Reynolds scored but the Black Demons' point-after try was low and wide. The Blackbirds won 14-13 to collect their fourth straight state title in the high-profile sports.

Rocky Mount used the halfback pass three times in the game and gained eighty-four yards on it. The Blackbirds threw for 210 yards total and ran for sixty.

"Our coaches felt Reynolds would make a real commitment on defense to stopping our running game," Laughridge says. "We put that pass in to counter any success they might have and keep them honest. I don't remember a tight spiral, but Jeff was so open it really didn't matter. It was a set-up and they took the bait. It was good coaching and good planning and excellent play-calling by Jimmy."

"Those crazy passes beat us," Reynolds coach Red Wilson lamented. "We knew they could throw the football, but not that well. That double pass was something new. It wasn't in any of the films we saw or in the scouting report."

The team spent the night in Winston-Salem, then returned early the next morning to Rocky Mount. Carpenter and athletic director Bill Lundy had made arrangements to take the players through Durham and watch the Carolina-Duke football game, but all college games scheduled that Saturday had been postponed because of the passing of President Kennedy.

"The President's death had a dampening effect on what would have been a pure celebration," Parker says. "He was a fairly popular guy among our age group. He was a young, attractive president. Still, there was reason to celebrate. We felt like we'd accomplished a huge amount that year. We had some rough spots early in the year and we worked hard to come together as a team. We had a good team at the end of the year. We proved we were a good team without Danny Talbott."

Bert Carter was a sophomore at Rocky Mount that year and remembers sitting in his homeroom early in the afternoon, waiting for the bell to dismiss everyone so they could travel to Winston-Salem.

"Suddenly the volume on the school's intercom system was turned up and we started hearing Walter Cronkite report the events from Dallas," says Carter, a member of the Class of 1966 and today a resident of Cary. "We were stunned. The trip to Winston-Salem was silent except for the news reports on the car radio. There wasn't much cheering at the game. We were numb."

A welcome reception planned for 6 p.m at the high school was cancelled, but a crowd estimated at 800 nonetheless gathered to meet the team upon its return.

"After the tragedy this nation suffered yesterday in the loss of President Kennedy, I don't think we should have expected a crowd as big as this," superintendent D.S. Johnson said. "People just aren't in a festive mood, despite the wonderful accomplishments of these boys."

The 1964 team was outstanding as well and was built around twenty-five seniors. The Blackbirds rolled through the season with a 10-0 record and captured Rocky Mount's third straight Eastern 4-A Conference title. Carpenter thinks it was the best of the three championship teams. But Arrington and Lundy were hurt against Wilson and lost for the rest of the year. Darrell Johnson took over at quarterback but, despite his considerable athletic skills, lacked the passing and field generalship abilities of Arrington. Opponents were able to key on Laughridge and the Rocky Mount offense sputtered late in the year. The Blackbirds lost to eventual champion Reynolds 14-7 in the state semifinals.

"We had nine players off that team earn scholarships," Carpenter says. "That was more than the other two teams."

"When we lost Arrington and Lundy in the Wilson game, we had to do so many modifications," Laughridge says. "I remember the last game of the year, at Raleigh Broughton, everywhere I went, they had two linebackers on me. We lost our balance and flexibility. If we could have stayed healthy, I don't think there was a team in the state that could have stood with us."

The basketball and baseball teams had average seasons in 1963-64. That spring, Carpenter was offered a job on coach Jim Hickey's staff at Carolina. As much as he and his family loved Rocky Mount, the limited ability to make outside income to supplement his teaching and coaching salaries made the college offer attractive. Carpenter left the high school ranks with a 51-13-3 record and five playoff appearances in his six years at Rocky Mount. Over the next two decades, he coached at UNC, Vanderbilt and Georgia Tech before moving into private business in the early 1970s. Today he lives in Florence, S.C., where he is retired and pursues his passion of owning and breeding horses.

"It was just a fun time," Carpenter says of the early 1960s days. "It was easy. The coaches worked hard, the players worked hard. We all got along great. To my knowledge, there was no jealousy on anyone's part. We were just having a good time coaching a bunch of good boys, trying our best to win." ∎

1963 BLACKBIRD FOOTBALL

Sept. 6	Henderson	20-0	H
Sept. 13	Kinston	0-7	A
Sept. 20	Goldsboro	13-0	A
Sept. 27	Wilmington	26-6	A
Oct. 4	Fayetteville	20-13	H
Oct. 11	Wilson	42-0	A
Oct. 18	Durham	13-6	H
Oct. 25	Greenville	35-0	H
Nov. 1	Myers Park	0-6	A
Nov. 8	Raleigh Broughton	6-0	H

State Playoffs

| Nov. 15 | Greensboro Page | 42-0 | H |
| Nov. 22 | W-S Reynolds | 14-13 | A |

Steve Kelly (40) and Wayne Daughtridge (26) converge on a Durham High ball carrier during a season in which the Blackbird defense allowed only 51 points over 12 games and notched six shutouts.

1963 State 4-A Champions

Front Row (L-R): Lee Pearce, Steve Britt, Steve Kelly, Craig Quick, Allen Ricks, Bill Bonner.

Second Row: Robbie Sykes, Brent Milgrom, Garry Brown, Bunn Woodard, Ivan Bunn, Lee Tyler, Wayne Daughtridge, Ronnie Herring.

Third Row: Jeff Croom, Clarence Lamm, Monk Reams, Mike Branch, Digit Laughridge, Jimmy Arrington, Don Rabon, Bobby Mills, Wesley Ballou.

Fourth Row: Jerry Lundy, Joe Swaim, Billy Warren, Skip Thompson, John Alexander, Bill Blaylock, Mike Boykin, Darrell Johnson, Don Bennett.

Fifth Row: Warren Broughton, Henry Strickland, Jimmy Clack, Bennett Lancaster, Ronald Barnes, Freddy Goblett, David Parker, J.W. Turner, J.C.. Warren.

CHARLES S. KILLEBREW COLLECTION, BRASWELL MEMORIAL LIBRARY

East Vs. West

Every fall the Blackbirds played a core of rivals in the Eastern 4-A Conference and a smattering of schools from neighboring towns like Tarboro and Kinston. Athletic director Bill Lundy had the notion as the program of coach Chris Carpenter matured that it might be fun and productive for Rocky Mount to venture beyond the confines of Eastern North Carolina.

Lundy talked to Gus Purcell, the head coach from 1951-71 at Myers Park High in Charlotte, in early 1961 and presented the idea of a home-and-home series between two of the state's top 4-A teams.

East versus west.

Dueling quarterbacks in the persons of Danny Talbott of Rocky Mount and Jeff Beaver of Myers Park.

Tobacco town challenges metropolitan suburbia.

"Our program was starting to get pretty good, and coach Lundy wanted us to expand beyond the six or seven teams we played every year in the conference," says Carpenter, the Blackbirds' head coach from 1959-64. "He approached me and I liked the idea. I thought it would be a great challenge for our kids."

Rocky Mount and Myers Park met during the regular season from 1961-66 and for a second time during the 1962 season in the state playoffs. Rocky Mount won the first three games and then Myers Park bounced back for a win in 1963. The Blackbirds were back on the winning path in 1964 with a 26-7 win. The schools played twice more in the series, with Myers Park winning the last two—27-7 in 1965 and 41-13 in 1966.

To save money and add to the cultural experience, the administrators arranged for the visiting teams to stay in the homes of the host team. After the games, the hosts

Blackbird offensive linemen pause from preparations for the 1962 playoff game against Myers Park (L-R): Dennis Newell, Bobby Jones, David Parker, Wayne Bulluck, Steve Wright, John Alexander and Bob Sides.
PHOTO COURTESY NORMA PARKER

took the visitors out on the town or, in the case of the 1961 game at Myers Park, arranged dates for the Blackbird players for a post-game sock hop. Brent Milgrom, a Rocky Mount defensive end and later a teammate of Beaver's at the University of North Carolina, remembers his host taking him to the South 21 Drive-In and a beach music haunt on South Boulevard called the Cave.

"When I got to Chapel Hill for orientation in August of '64, we met under the Davie Poplar, and one of the ten or so students there was Ken Cameron, my host from Myers Park," Milgrom says. "We became good friends. Later I loaned him my letter jacket when he wanted to impress his date."

"It was an interesting time and a fun experience," says Beaver, who was the quarterback of Myers Park's robust passing offense in 1961 and '62. "It turns out several of their players went to Carolina with me. Danny I were competitors and good friends. We even double-dated a couple of nurses our freshman year. Wrennie Pitt and I were fraternity brothers. And Brent now lives in Charlotte and I see him frequently.

"But at the time, we were just young kids playing football. The Rocky Mount games expanded our world. I remember that drive to Rocky Mount on the bus took forever."

"The road trips were a lot of fun," guard David Parker says. "We enjoyed those. It was a big deal to put on your blazer and tie and go a big town somewhere, to Charlotte or Winston-Salem. The build-up for those games was huge."

Milgrom was impressed by the tall buildings of the Charlotte skyline and the dozens and dozens of players the Mustangs dressed out. Rocky Mount, meanwhile, had a traveling squad of thirty-four.

"It was like playing a small-college team," Milgrom says. "Another thing I remember is all the Myers Park players came out for warm-ups and they were wearing

Beaver (L) and Talbott teamed as Tar Heels after two years of high school matchups.

matching green and white toboggans."

The hats were known as "Beaver-boggans" as Beaver's mother knitted them for each player.

"We were really into the pro system, from the passing game to warm-ups," says Beaver, today the executive director of the Charlotte Sports Commission. "Coach Purcell would watch the Redskins games on Sunday afternoon and draw up plays off the TV, this being long before VCRs. But he could watch a play one time and then draw up what every player did.

"Something else the pros did was to come out for warm-ups, to throw and catch and kick, before the whole team came out together. Coach let us do that as well. So we'd come out without our shoulder pads and helmets. On cold nights, we all wore our tobaggans."

Julian Fenner, a tackle on the 1962-63 teams, remembers playing on a cold night in Charlotte when the painted stripes on the field were so cold they were like white bricks.

"We were in awe of their professionalism," Fenner says. "As we came running onto the field, pretty much everyone on our team tripped over those yard lines and fell down. It was almost comical. Of course, we wound up winning the game and redeeming ourselves."

Purcell decided in the late '50s that he would build his offense around the quarterback. The Mustangs threw the ball often and used a variety of gadget plays.

"We had a triple-reverse pass, a flea-flicker, a hidden-ball trick and a couple of halfback passes," Beaver says. "The players loved it, the fans loved it. Guys a couple of years ahead of my class would come back home from college to see us play. What we were doing was a lot more interesting than what the college teams were doing."

Myers Park tried a trick play in the 1962 game where an end acts as if he's leaving the game and lures the cornerback on his side of the field into losing track of him. Digit Laughridge was playing left corner and watched a Mustang player supposedly leave the game. He looked back to the quarterback, watched the snap and saw Beaver looking directly at him and slinging the football.

"I thought, 'Who's he throwing to?'" Laughridge says. "The guy never left the game and was wide open behind me. Fortunately, Beaver overthrew him. I learned a lesson I never forgot. From then on, all the way through Wake Forest, if a guy was leaving the game, I made sure he *left* the game."

The Rocky Mount-Myers Park games featured contrasting styles, with the Mustangs throwing the ball at will and the Blackbirds' strengths built around stout defense and the all-around running, throwing and generalship skills of Talbott.

The 1961 game was held in Charlotte, the ninth game

of the year for both teams. Myers Park was 6-2, having lost its first two games but then reeling off six wins in a row. Rocky Mount was 7-0-1. Both teams were ranked in the top five in the state in separate polls run by *The Charlotte Observer* and *The Charlotte News*.

Beaver, a junior, became the starting quarterback in the fifth game when Jim Rogers was injured. In three games, Beaver had completed fifty-nine of 114 passes for 766 yards and seven touchdowns. Rocky Mount leaned more toward a ground attack as Talbott had attempted only eighty-three passes for the entire year, completing thirty-nine for 674 yards and eight scores.

Rocky Mount won the game, 21-18, taking a two-touchdown lead and holding off a late Mustang rally. Myers Park converted two onsides kicks in the fourth quarter before a late interception preserved the Blackbirds' victory.

Talbott churns for yards against Myers Park in 27-14 win in 1962; two weeks later, the Blackbirds traveled to Charlotte to beat the Mustangs in the playoffs.

The two schools played twice in 1962. Myers Park returned the home game and traveled to Rocky Mount in the ninth game of the regular season. Then they met again two weeks later in the first round of the playoffs (at the time there were only two playoff games).

Both teams were 7-0-1 when they kicked off in Rocky Mount in a game touted by one newspaper as a "battle of illustrious quarterbacks." Beaver had thrown 178 passes in eight games (completing seventy-eight for 1,335 yards), while Talbott had launched only sixty-eight (connecting on twenty-nine for 319 yards). But the Blackbirds were churning out 292 yards a game of total offense, 222 on the ground and seventy passing.

Rocky Mount won 27-14 as Talbott threw for one score, ran for another and accounted for a third on a fourth-quarter interception returned into the end zone.

"They are the best team I have seen," Purcell said.

"They are well-balanced and beat you many ways. Talbott does everything. He's the boy who makes Rocky Mount go."

The playoff game drew 8,834 fans to Memorial Stadium in Charlotte, and Carpenter's plan was to continue to play keep-away from Beaver and his bevy of talented receivers like Byron Slaughter and Bud Phillips. Rocky Mount won, 21-6, then went on to beat Winston-Salem Reynolds for the first of two straight football titles.

Talbott and Beaver both played at Carolina and entered Chapel Hill in the fall of 1963. Talbott was drafted by San Francisco in the 17th round of the 1967 NFL draft following his senior season in 1966. Beaver had been red-shirted and played one more year in '67 and was a fifteenth-round selection by the Baltimore Colts. Talbott first tried a year of professional baseball, but after the 49ers traded his rights to the Washington Redskins a year later, he decided in the summer of 1968 to give pro football a shot. Beaver's Colts played Talbott's Redskins in a rookie game before the 1968 season.

"We played in Memorial Stadium in Baltimore," Beaver remembers. "I had a real good game. And that was the first and only time I ever beat Danny Talbott." ∎

Epilogue

With many there is one salient recollection, one odd or end that sticks in their memory bank when they reflect on the halcyon days of Blackbird athletics from the early 1960s, that run of four state titles from football in 1962 through football the following autumn.

For Bill Warren, it's the Pepsi Colas from the ice buckets immediately after football practice.

"The best drink I've ever had in my life were those iced-down Pepsi Colas right after practice," Warren says. "Back then you didn't drink water. They gave you a few sips to survive, but you didn't get much. So when we came off the field we were dehydrated. You'd sit down in the shade and drink those Pepsis and it was just about the most refreshing thing I've ever tasted. To this day I still drink Pepsi."

For Jim Daniels, it's the sting in his mitt hand after catching Danny Talbott for seven innings on the baseball field.

"Danny had good control and wasn't that hard to catch," says Daniels, the catcher on the 1963 state baseball championship team. "It just *hurt* to catch him. He was overpowering. I can close my eyes and still feel it. I'm telling you, it was something else."

Marion Barnes remembers leading a group of football players in stealing coach Chris Carpenter's tires used for practice drills, setting them on fire and getting nabbed by the police. He also reflects fondly on a late-night dinner and celebration prepared for the team upon its return from Raleigh after a big win in 1962. David Lamm remembers soaking a towel in cold water, stuffing it under his shoulder pads and sucking the towel for a few drops of

"HI-NOC-AR" YEARBOOK PHOTO

water during hot August football practices. "By then, though, it was half sweat and half water," he says. Steve Wright remembers finding a box full of bottles of aftershave a decade after Rocky Mount merchants lavished victorious Blackbirds with all manner of gifts.

"It really was a time when the planets, timing, skills, individuals and coaching aligned," says Digit Laughridge, a Blackbird in football and baseball from 1962-65. "Considering we were the smallest 4-A school in the state, it was truly remarkable. I wish I could remember every detail, but it comes and goes—and I wouldn't trade a minute of it for anything."

"It was a point in time with the right people in the right setting, and all the puzzle pieces fell perfectly into place," adds Tom Parrish, a senior on the first football title team and on the 1963 basketball championship squad. "And all of us became better people because of the experience."

Bob Williams was sports editor of the *Rocky Mount Telegram* in the 1950s and '60s and covered every football and basketball game and many baseball games. He also knew many of the players from having coached them in YMCA youth league games in the 1950s. He left the newspaper business in 1973 to join his family's Rocky Mount construction business, Central Builders Inc. Today he marvels at the significance of the accomplishment. One North Carolina high school, Robert Marson High of Raleigh, won the football, basketball and baseball titles in 1935-36, but its string stopped at three. No school has dominated the football-basketball-baseball triumvirate to the same degree since Rocky Mount's 1962-63 miracle run.

"If I could live through that again, I would *live* it, because we didn't, not really," Williams says. "We enjoyed it, but it passed by, but we didn't really *live* it. We didn't understand what was happening. The people of Rocky Mount, including myself, did not realize just what an accomplishment this was. If I could do it again, I would really *live* it, each person, each coach, each game. I would let it absorb me. Today I can realize just what it was this town accomplished."

Nearly half a century has passed and Blackbirds have dispersed to all manner of lives, careers and accomplishments. Along with their memories, they've taken lessons and values into adulthood.

"Don't quit. Do *not* be a quitter," says Barnes, who owns and operates Frontier Trailer Associates, a tank trailer dealership in Rocky Mount. "Life is not always easy. You have to get off the floor. Business ventures, personal stuff knocks you down sometimes. You might feel like quitting, but you don't."

Barnes ran seven marathons in the 1980s and ran his first New York City Marathon in 1984, finishing in three hours, thirty-eight minutes.

"Turning on Central Park South to the finish line, I didn't think I would make it," Barnes says. "My mind went back to the fifteen-minute squad on Chris Carpenter's practice field. *You better not quit.* It was the same thing at Quantico in the Marines. We did these twenty-mile 'forced marches.' I was the platoon leader. It was a cold February day. Your feet were freezing and you had blisters from those boots. I kept thinking back to high school. That experience pulled me through."

Warren lives in Raleigh and is a business owner and automotive consultant.

"One of the things I learned is a saying, 'It's amazing what you can accomplish when you don't care who gets the credit,'" he says. "I think we had a very unselfish team. I mean, we all liked to see our names in the headlines and that stuff, but there wasn't any jealousy. We were a very close-knit, team-oriented deal."

Laughridge lives in Campobello, S.C., and is sales and marketing director for Bommer Industries, a worldwide manufacturer of construction hardware.

"You can't have prima donnas and have a successful

team," he says. "You can't let personal pride get in the way of a team objective. The coaches kept us pretty damn humble. We were lucky enough to see that type of approach to anything can be extremely successful."

Jep Rose graduated from Davidson College in 1969, the University of North Carolina School of Law in 1972 and today is an attorney and partner in the Rocky Mount law firm Poyner & Spruill.

"You learned the importance of teamwork," he says. "You had to work together to accomplish the common goal. It taught you a lot about not being selfish. I've experienced the 'corporate high' of winning a big case, celebrating with others, knowing it came about because you worked together. You also learned that you've got to go along sometimes with things you disagree with. Once you make the decision, you go with it—unless it's something you think is illegal or immoral."

Parker graduated from N.C. State University in 1968, then from Harvard Business School in 1971 and has been in the investment banking business for most of his working life. Today he lives in Greensboro and is managing director of Triangle Capital Corporation in Raleigh.

"We learned the importance of preparation," he says. "You learned how to devote the hours of preparation into two hours of competition. You can't just show up on Fridays and play. The same principle applies in business."

Dudley Whitley spent thirty-three years in coaching, teaching and administration in the Rocky Mount school system and marveled at the positive influence a winning sports program had on the broad school operation.

"I've been in education all my life," says Whitley, retired now and living in Rocky Mount. "Successful athletics make for successful schools. It carries over. When you win, you do well in school. You have fewer problems. Kids take pride in their entire school operation. Success in athletics leads to success in other areas."

Carpenter, the head football coach from 1959-64, says there is no doubt that the job of Rocky Mount Senior High principal Cy Edson became easier when the Blackbirds were winning.

"I understand problems went down when football went up," Carpenter says. "All the problems went the other way. Athletics did that. When I got to Rocky Mount, there was more mess going on than you could shake a stick at. Athletics carried the tone of the entire school. I know that, there is no question about it.

"Everyone took pride in what we were doing. The students had fun with what we were doing. They came to the games because we were winning. When students left and went on to college, I know they took pride in saying, 'I'm from Rocky Mount Senior High.'" ■

Darrell Johnson runs from his halfback position for yardage against Greenville.

Darrell Johnson

I spent the entire afternoon alone in Wait Chapel on the Wake Forest campus when I got the message Darrell was missing. The last time we saw each other on the field, we were on our freshman teams when Wake played South Carolina in Columbia. I still remember tackling him one-on-one on a punt return and each of us laughing, grabbing each other and banging face masks at the end of the play. The last time I saw him at all was back in Rocky Mount on break one weekend, just before he went off with the Special Forces. I can see him vividly in my mind and I can write these words ... I simply can't speak them. We were always together on both sides of the ball and instinctively knew what the other was doing. He was like a brother off the field, and I still miss him after all these years. And that's just the way it will be for me, until I see him again."

Digit Laughridge via email, August 27, 2007

Sergeant 1st Class Darrell Johnson and his squad were exchanging fire in early 1968 with Vietcong troops in the central highlands of Vietnam near the Cambodia and Laos borders, some forty miles northwest of the town of Dak To. Johnson was last seen alive in a tree, firing his weapon at the enemy. The bodies of the rest of his squad members were found, but Johnson's never was. He is listed as "Missing in Action."

"Darrell was so special. He was probably the most liked player on any of our teams," says Bill Warren, who was one year ahead of Johnson at Rocky Mount Senior High. "I was with him the last night he was home. We told each other goodbye at about five in the morning before he went to get on a plane to Nam."

Laughridge lived with his grandparents during high school, just two blocks from the Johnson family. Laughridge and Johnson were starters in the offensive and defensive backfields and on the baseball field throughout their careers.

"Darrell had all the tools," Laughridge says. "He was reasonably tall, swift and quick. Everyone had a kind of confidence that if Darrell's number was called, he was going to execute the play and pick up some yards."

Johnson enjoyed some early notoriety in athletics, pitching a no-hitter as a ten-year-old on the Rotary Club team in the YMCA youth league. He was particularly fond of football and baseball and staved off his mother's concerns about the dangers of football by saying, "Momma, if I get killed playing football, you'll know I died happy."

After that, says Mildred Johnson, "I didn't say any more."

Johnson was most valuable player in football and baseball during his senior year of 1964-65. He was to Rocky Mount Senior High what "The Fonz" was to the *Happy Days* gang—long sideburns and plenty of cool. He had a dry sense of humor and was a master of the understatement.

Playing quarterback during the 1964 season, Johnson occasionally mixed up some elements of the offensive play call. When a teammate would offer the correct formation or signal call, Johnson would agree by saying, "Yeah, all that jazz." Once in a tight game, Laughridge interjected during a huddle call and Johnson looked reproachfully at his pal.

"Digit, just get us a touchdown!" Johnson ordered.

Laughridge scored and Johnson pulled him out of the ensuing pile in the end zone. Johnson grinned and said, "See, told ya!'"

"From then on," Laughridge says, "anyone on the team who forgot what they were trying to say would dismiss it with a flip of the hand and say, 'You know, all that jazz.'"

Johnson earned a scholarship to the University of South Carolina and played one year of freshman ball. He entered the Army Special Forces in November 1967. One of his favorite songs, ironically, was a number by country/blues singer Joe Tex entitled *I Believe I'm Gonna Make It;* the ballad tells of a soldier's love for his girlfriend and his hope to return home soon from Vietnam.

Nearly four decades after the incident on Jan. 19, 1968, the loss of Johnson leaves a void in many lives.

"It's an unfinished part of my life," says Bill Higgs, a suitemate of Johnson's at South Carolina in 1965. "I've never gotten over it. A lot of people haven't."

"I can almost cry," says Charlie Daniels, the long-time leader of the Rocky Mount YMCA youth sports programs. "I drive past his old house often. It's three blocks from my house. I go by and think he walked out that door and never walked back in."

Each Christmas Eve, on the anniversary of Johnson's birth in 1946, Marion Barnes visits Mildred Johnson. The first two things Mrs. Johnson does is show Barnes the Christmas card she receives from The White House and the card and family photo she gets each year from Laughridge, who lives in Campobello, S.C. They look at the last photo taken of Darrell, and Barnes invariably remarks that Johnson "stole" the necktie he's wearing from Barnes.

"I feel better and she feels better," Barnes says. "Still, I know her heart's broken. Your's would be too if your son fell off the face of the earth and you still don't know what happened." ∎

Blackbird Legacy

The following poem was written by Jim Daniels, the catcher on the 1963 baseball team, and is dedicated "to all the coaches and players on the Blackbird teams who made such a great run possible, with special mention on behalf of those no longer with us: Darrell Johnson, Jimmy Coats, Eddie Allen, manager Kenneth Rackley, Jimmy Clack, Coach C.V. Lundy, Coach Jimmy Armstrong and Purvis Edwards."

A great sports story is waiting to be told,
About teams of Blackbirds in days of old,
It was the fall of '62 when it all began,
Through the fall of '63, that the streak ran,
Four straight 4A State Championships show,
That truly great coaches and players won four in a row,
Football came first, a cut above the rest,
The Rocky Mount Blackbirds were by far the best,
Then came basketball and the struggle was great,
But our "Dear Senior High," destiny could not wait,
Baseball and the boys of spring came along,
Glory be! A third title was our song,
Finally to the amazement of all concerned,
Football again came along and again we won,
Pride and honor is what I feel,
For my small part on the baseball field.
All coaches and players alike, I am sure,
Have a lifetime memory that will always endure,
Our destiny was a powerful motivator to heed,
Rocky Mount Senior High Blackbirds were special indeed!

Jimmy Clack

Jimmy Clack was a winner. He knew how to win from his days playing football and basketball at Rocky Mount Senior High, when the Blackbirds collected two state titles in football and one in basketball. His legacy as a champion evolved with two Super Bowl rings earned as a center with the Pittsburgh Steelers in the mid-1970s.

So in 1978, when New York Giants owner Wellington Mara and first-year coach Ray Perkins were looking for players to help arrest two decades' worth of losing, players with pedigrees like Clack's were their building blocks.

"We needed someone to teach us to be a winner, and Jimmy was that guy," says Harry Carson, a Hall of Fame Giants linebacker and Clack teammate. "He helped us learn to be winners. He had a winning attitude, and he infused that to the rest of the guys, particularly on offense. He was the one guy with the positive mentality that affected everyone else."

Added Perkins: "Jim was one of the greatest leaders I have ever been around in all my years coaching."

Clack died of heart failure in April 2006 following a four-year battle with neck and throat cancer. He was fifty-eight. After retiring from the NFL following the 1981 season, Clack developed a multi-faceted business career. He was a restaurateur; a commercial and residential real estate developer; and a consultant and motivational speaker to a variety of businesses.

"Jimmy was a quiet yeoman," says Digit Laughridge, a football teammate at Rocky Mount and then at Wake Forest from 1966-68. "He would not say 'Boo,' but he would not give up for anything. He was a big, raw-boned kid. He wasn't a hoot-and-holler kind of guy, but he'd

No. 50 as a Wake Forest Demon Deacon in the 1960s and a Pittsburgh Steeler in the 1970s.

knock you on your rear end. He just loved the game."

Clack played cymbals in the school band early in his teen-age years, but his size attracted the attention of the coaches, who encouraged him to try out for athletics. He developed quickly enough to play varsity football and basketball during his sophomore year of 1962-63.

"He had all kinds of determination," says Bob Kornegay, a lifelong friend and a 1966 Rocky Mount graduate. "He got good coaching, and Lord knows we had the best coaching in the world at that time. He had a lot of good athletes around him to challenge him and bring out his best. He started getting bigger and stronger and made a name for himself."

Clack played center on offense and linebacker on defense; he returned an interception ninety-five yards for a touchdown in the season opener against Henderson in 1963. He was a center in basketball; his rebound and follow shot at the buzzer provided the winning points in the Blackbirds' 52-50 win over Greensboro Grimsley in winning the 1963 state title. And to remain active during the spring, Clack was an excellent field athlete with the shot put and discus.

Clack (kneeling on left) celebrates with teammates and coaches after game-winning basket over Greensboro Grimsley.

Clack joined teammates Laughridge and Jimmy Arrington in accepting scholarship offers from coach Bill Tate at Wake Forest. He started for three years, playing linebacker for two and then moving to offensive tackle for his senior year in 1968. One of his best games was his defensive performance in a 3-0 win at UNC in 1966.

Clack had nine tackles in the second half and recovered a fumble at the ten yard line in the fourth quarter as the Deacons thwarted a Tar Heel scoring threat. Fellow

Rocky Mount alumnus Danny Talbott, a two-sport star in Chapel Hill, did not play in that game until the fourth quarter because of a sprained ankle.

"Jimmy played like a man possessed," Laughridge says. "Rocky Mount was a Carolina town, and for the three of us to go against the grain and go to Wake Forest made the Carolina games a big deal for us. They were for bragging rights and pride."

The 215-pound Clack signed with the Steelers as a free agent in 1969 and was the last player cut and sent to the "taxi squad" at the end of training camp that year and again in 1970. But he never gave up and continued to work to develop his size and strength. Kornegay remembers Clack had gained thirty pounds when he came home to Rocky Mount for Christmas after one of those early years with the Steelers.

"He was wearing a Lacoste shirt and his biceps and arms and shoulders were humongous," Kornegay says. "He looked like the Hulk. He became much more agile and powerful."

Clack paid his dues and moved into the starting offensive line that blocked for Terry Bradshaw and Franco Harris during runs to Super Bowl titles following the 1974 and '75 seasons. He was endearing to his teammates for his courage and resolve, not to mention a sense of humor that was always on the prowl for a good practical joke. And in an era when whites and blacks were still learning to be friends, neighbors, teammates and equals, Clack was the lubricant in the locker room.

"He was like the liaison guy," says Kornegay, who visited Clack regularly in Pittsburgh. "The black guys liked him and trusted him. He fit in real well. He would have been a good union rep. He was a friend and was straight with everyone."

Clack felt his two knees had been banged up enough for one career after the 1981 season and announced his retirement. But he told Perkins, "If you need me, give me a call." The Giants had serious injury problems and Perkins did in fact call Clack in early November; he suited up and played in emergency duty against Dallas, then played six more weeks as the Giants made the playoffs for the first time in eighteen years.

When Carson learned of Clack's death, he made arrangements to attend Clack's services in Greensboro, where Clack lived following his NFL career.

"His work ethic stands out in my mind," Carson says. "It was very clear he wanted to win. He was usually going up against bigger guys, and he utilized his speed, strength, leverage and, most importantly, his heart, to succeed on the field." ∎

Benefactors

[Brackets denote player's football jersey number] (Parentheses denote player's basketball jersey number)

Championship Sponsors

Don Stallings, Class of 1956 [64] (41) and baseball; Assistant Football Coach; by Stallings Oil Company.

In memory of Ruby and Henry Milgrom, by Brent Milgrom Family Foundation, Inc.

Jep Rose, Class of 1964 [66] (35), track and Sheep's Club.

The Sheep's Club—Body, Edwardo, Esque, Mayor, Monkey, Red, Root Nose, Skipee, Spick, Sportsman, Tiger, White Whale.

Touchdown Sponsors

In honor of Brent Milgrom [88], track and Sheep's Club, by Brent Milgrom, Jr., Family.

Chuck Robbins, Class of 1964 (15), by COECO Office Systems.

E. Allen Wester, Class of 1963 [77] (55).

In memory of my friend Darrell Johnson—MIA Vietnam, Class of 1965 [30] and baseball, by Digit Laughridge [33] and baseball.

Marion Barnes, Class of 1963 [80].

Ted Ward, Class of 1966, and Jackie Page Ward, Class of 1968.

Thomas A. Betts Jr., Class of 1959.

Field Goal Sponsors

Ann Milgrom Kennedy, Class of 1966, varsity cheerleader.

Annie Justa Alperin, Class of 1963, accompanist for choir, Good Sports Club.

Bill and Lindy Brice Blaylock, Class of 1965; Bill [84]; Lindy cheerleader.

Bill Warren, Class of 1963 [86] (33), and baseball.

Bob Marshburn, Class of 1964, tennis.

Bobby and Judy Gatling Morgan; Bobby Class of 1967, Judy Class of 1969.

Bobby and Debbie Slone Kornegay, Jr.; Debbie Class of 1967 and cheerleader; Bobby Class of 1966 [64].

In honor of Brent Milgrom, by Ann Cass and Sophie, daughter and grand-daughter.

In memory of Carol Mortimer, Class of 1964, varsity cheerleader, by Janice Mortimer Perdue.

Craig and Mimi Munden Quick, Class of 1964; Mimi, majorette; Craig [11] and baseball.

In memory of Darrell Johnson, MIA Vietnam, Class of 1965 [30] and baseball, by Mickey Southerland.

David and Jackie Redding Williams, Class of 1963; David, track; Jackie, head majorette.

Dillon Rose, Class of 1966 [26](31), track and Sheep's Club.

Don and Becky Bulluck Bennett; Becky Class of 1965, Don Class of 1964 [68]

Dudley Whitley, Class of 1952, three-sport letterman; teacher, head baseball coach, football coach, basketball coach.

Eddie Baysden, Class of 1966 [30], Sheep's Club.

Edward Arrington, Class of 1963, Public Speaking and S.O.S. Clubs.

Ernest Bridgers, Class of 1961 [47].

Frank and Josephine Vann Harrison; Josephine, Class of 1966, cheerleader; Frank, Class of 1965, (34) and Sheep's Club.

Frank Wilson, Class of 1961.

Gene Phipps, Class of 1965, golf.

Gus Tulloss, Class of 1961 [32].

Jack Cummings Jr, Class of 1964, Co-Editor, "HI-NOC-AR."

Jim Daniels, Jr., Class of 1963, baseball.

In honor of my friend, Lee Pearce, Jr. [66] by Jimmy Hagan.

Joe Philips, Class of 1964 [50 & 54]

John Alexander, Class of 1964 [76] and golf.

Julian Fenner, Class of 1964 [78] and Sheep's Club.

Lee Pearce, Jr., Class of 1965 [66].

Marshall Henry, Class of 1964, Blackbird communicator and Sheep's Club.

Martha Weeks Daniel, Class of 1962, Editor, "HI-NOC-AR."

In memory of Mike Branch, Class of 1964 [22] and Sheep's Club, by Joe Philips.

Nancy Severance Haynes, Class of 1964, Good Sports Club.

In memory of Robby Sykes, Class of 1965 [72], by Martha Hale Sykes Proctor.

Robert Bridgers, Class of 1963 [44].

Robert Ricks, Class of 1963 [26] (13).

Silas "Doubie" Snow, Class of 1960 [54] and baseball.

Skip Thompson, Class of 1964 [89], baseball and Sheep's Club.

Wade Pitt, Class of 1964.

In memory of Woody Brown, Class of 1962 [54], by Mickey Southerland.

William Milgrom, Class of 1961 [65].

Wrennie Pitt, Class of 1963 [22], track.

Powder-Puff time at Rocky Mount Senior High, Circa 1963.
PHOTO COURTESY NORMA PARKER